LUIGI PIRANDELLO

# Six Characters in Search of an Author

*translated by*
JOHN LINSTRUM

*with commentary and notes by*
JOSEPH FARRELL, *Professor of Italian, University of Strathclyde*

B L O O M S B U R Y
NEW DELHI • LONDON • OXFORD • NEW YORK • SYDNEY

First published in India 2014
This edition first published in the United Kingdom in 2004 by MethuenPublishing Ltd

Reissued with additional material and a new cover design 2006
Reissued with a new cover design 2009
Reprinted by Bloomsbury Methuen Drama 2010, 2013

This translation of *Six Characters in Search of an Author* first published in the United Kingdom by Eyre Methuen in 1979. Revised and reprinted by Methuen London in 1982


Originally published in Italian in 1921 as *Sei personaggi in cerca d'autore*


Bloomsbury Methuen Drama
An imprint of Bloomsbury Publishing Plc
Bloomsbury is a registered trade mark of Bloomsbury Publishing Plc

This edition published with permission from Bloosmbury Publishing Plc
50 Bedford Square, London, WC1B3DP



Cover design: Jocelyn Lucas


**British Library Cataloguing-in-Publication Data**
A catalogue record for this book is available from the British Library.

ISBN: PB: 978 93 84052 58 4
10 9 8

For sale in the Indian subcontinent only

MIX
Paper | Supporting responsible forestry
FSC® C191020

Bloomsbury Publishing India Pvt. Ltd
Second Floor, Building No.4
DDA Complex LSC, Pocket C – 6 & 7
Vasant Kunj, New Delhi 110070

**Library of Congress Cataloging-in-Publication Data**
A catalog record for this book is available from the Library of Congress.

Typeset by Deltatype Ltd, Birkenhead, Merseyside
Printed and bound in India by Gopsons Papers Pvt. Ltd., Noida

# Contents

# Luigi Pirandello: 1867–1936

1867 Luigi Pirandello born in a district called Caos, near Agrigento in the south of Sicily, where his pregnant mother had been forced to flee on account of an outbreak of cholera. Pirandello relished the irony of the place-name. 'I am then the child of Chaos, and not allegorically but in plain reality.' Sicily had been united with the rest of Italy only in 1860 when Giuseppe Garibaldi launched his invasion from the port of Marsala, overthrowing the Bourbon Kingdom of the Two Sicilies. The Pirandello family had been anti-Bourbon, and Pirandello's father, Stefano, had fought with Garibaldi.

1870s Childhood and schooling in Agrigento, a city whose Greek temples testified to its origins as an ancient Greek colony. Receives primary education at home, by a tutor he later satirised. Relations with his overbearing father distant and difficult. Banditry and mafia were unchecked forces in the region, and Stefano Pirandello was involved with duels and fights. The Pirandello family was relatively prosperous, due to their ownership of a sulphur mine, the main industry in pre-industrial Sicily. Luigi is given a conventional religious education, which he abandons in adolescence, blaming the hypocrisy of a priest who awarded him a prize he had not won so as to curry favour with his well-connected family. Also marked by an early experience of seeing a couple making love beside a coffin. Love and death will always be twinned forces in his work.

1878 Enrolled by his father in a technical college, to study mathematics in preparation for a business career. Luigi rebels, and enrols in another school to study classics.

1880 Stefano Pirandello goes bankrupt, leaving the family in penury. Move to Palermo, where Luigi continues his education. In his teens, falls in love with a neighbour, Giovanna. Contracts an illness which brings him close to death.

1881 Adulterous affair by Stefano Pirandello, leading to birth of an illegitimate child. Luigi, outraged, surprises the two together and spits on the woman. Coolness towards father increases.

1884 Publishes his first poem in a Turin newspaper.

1885 Sister Lina shows first symptoms of incipient insanity. Family moves to Porto Empedocle, near Agrigento. Luigi remains in Palermo, moves in with an elderly aunt. Falls in love with his cousin, also called Lina, four years older than him.

1886 Enrols in the Faculty of Literature and Law at the University of Palermo. Makes contact with the young rebels who will provide the leadership of a rural socialist movement known as *Fasci siciliani*.

1887 Becomes engaged to Lina. Under pressure from the family, leaves university to work in the sulphur mine with his father. Unsuited to office work, enrols at the University of Rome to study literature. Feelings for Lina begin to cool.

1889 Publishes in Palermo his first collection of poetry, *Mal giocondo*. Following a squabble at a lecture, is expelled from university. Moves to Germany to follow a course in Romance Philology at the University of Bonn. Returns to Sicily, for a meeting with an increasingly unhappy Lina to whom he is still officially engaged. Falls ill again.

1889–91 Residence in Bonn, perhaps the happiest period of his life. Deep relationship with Jenny Schulz-Lander.

1891 Publishes in Milan, at his father's expense, his second collection of poetry, *Pasqua di Gea*, dedicated to Jenny. Gains a doctorate from Bonn with a thesis on the dialects of his native Agrigento. Breaks his engagement with Lina, explaining his reasons in a self-serving letter to his father. Returns to Sicily, where his father promises him a monthly allowance. Ends his relationship with Jenny.

1892 Settles in Rome. With the help of fellow Sicilian writer, Luigi Capuana, makes contact with the literary élite of the capital, and establishes himself as a man of letters, publishing stories and articles. Writes his first play, a one-act piece *Why?*, unperformed during his lifetime.

1893 Writes his first novel *The Outcast Woman*, published only in 1901.

1894 In Sicily, weds Maria Antonietta Portulano, daughter of one of his father's business associates, in an arranged marriage. The two had met only briefly in the days preceding the wedding. Pirandello's wife brings a large dowry, and ownership of a sulphur mine. The couple set up home in Rome. Publishes first anthology of short stories, *Loves Without Love*. Devotes less time to poetry, more to fiction.

1895 First child, Stefano, born. Publishes new collection of verse, *Rhineland Elegies*, written during his time in Germany, inspired in part by Goethe's *Roman Elegies*, which he was then translating. Writes second novel, *The Turn*.

1897 Daughter, Lietta, born. Family finances strained. Takes up a job as teacher of Italian in a girls' school in Rome.

1898 Publishes new one-act play, later given the title *The Vice*. Signs of strain in relations with his wife, who exhibits the first symptoms of mental instability.

1899 Third child, Fausto, born.

1901 The two completed novels serialised in Roman periodicals.

1903 The sulphur mine in Sicily in which Stefano Pirandello had invested both his own money and his daughter-in-law's dowry is flooded, leaving both him and his son's family financially ruined. The disaster drives Maria Antonietta, whose mental state is already precarious, into insanity. She is also left, temporarily, semi-paralysed. Pirandello himself contemplates suicide. Later that year, publishes in serial form *The Late Mattia Pascal*, an immediate success and perhaps his greatest novel. Translated into German the following year.

1904 New collection of short stories, *Blacks and Whites*, appears. In spite of his growing fame, Pirandello's home life is desperately unhappy, as his wife sinks further into jealous paranoia, accusing him endlessly, and mistakenly, of infidelity. Pirandello refuses to heed those who suggest that she requires care in a mental hospital.

1906 Two collections of short stories, *Jokes of Life and Death* and *When I Was Mad* . . ., appear.

1908 Two important essays, 'Art and Science' and 'On Humour', published, partly to help win promotion and an increased salary in his educational career.

1909 Sections of his only historical novel, *The Old and the Young*, set in post-Risorgimento Sicily, published in magazine. Completed work published in 1913. Condition of Maria Antonietta continues to deteriorate, with occasional outbursts of violence.

1910 First theatrical productions. The Sicilian actor-author-director, Nino Martoglio, stages two one-act plays, *Limes of Sicily* and *The Vice*, both adapted from short stories, establishing a pattern of adaptation from his own work which Pirandello will follow throughout his life.

1911 Novel *Her Husband* published.

1912 Volume of short stories, *Tercets*, and final collection of poems, *Off Key*, published.

1913 A further one-act play, *The Doctor's Duty*, also adapted from a previous short story, staged in Rome. The continuing need to provide medical care for his wife imposes severe financial burdens on

Pirandello, who is obliged to seek loans from Nino Martoglio with the promise of providing a film script for a company Martoglio is directing.

1915 First full-length play, *If Not So* (later retitled *Other People's Reasons*), premièred in Milan. Discouraged by the lukewarm response, Pirandello decides to write no more for the stage. New novel *Shoot!*, set in cinema world, serialised. Two volumes of short stories published and one-act play, *Cecè*, staged. Italy enters First World War, and Pirandello's son, Stefano, enlists. Captured by the Austrians, spends the rest of the war as POW, to Pirandello's immense distress. His mother dies in Sicily. His father, alone, infirm and half-blind, moves in with his daughter Lina, also resident in Rome, with Pirandello paying the bulk of the costs.

1916 Coaxed back to the theatre, collaborates with the company of the famous Sicilian actor, Angelo Musco, who stages two works, *Think It Over, Giacomino* and the dialect play, *Liolà*. Maria Antonietta develops the paranoid belief that her husband and daughter have an incestuous relationship and are plotting to poison her. Lietta attempts suicide. She leaves the family home for Florence.

1917 Musco stages *Cap and Bells*, and later *The Jar*. Pirandello receives recognition as a playwright of national standing, whom the leading companies of the day vie with one another to stage. Virginio Talli premières *Right You Are! (If You Think So)* in Milan, and Ruggero Ruggeri stars in *The Pleasure of Honesty* in Turin.

1918 *But It's Not a Serious Matter* premièred in Livorno, and *The Rules of the Game* in Rome. The end of the war leads to Stefano's release from the prisoner-of-war camp.

1919 Maria Antonietta is committed to a mental hospital, where she remains until her death in 1959. Lietta returns to the family home. *Man, the Beast and Virtue* premièred in Milan. Two other volumes of short stories, *Berecche and the War* and *Carnival of the Dead*, published. First encounter with cinema for filming of *But It's Not a Serious Matter.*

1920 *As Well as Before, Better than Before* produced in Venice, and *Mrs Morli, One and Two* premièred in Rome. Pirandello's new publisher, Mondadori, begins to publish the plays under the overall title *Naked Masks*, and the collected short fiction under the general title *Tales for a Year.*

1921 *Six Characters in Search of an Author* premièred in May in Rome, where the baffled audience riots. Pirandello forced to take refuge from a mob who stand waiting for him outside the theatre. The second production in September in Milan is a triumph, gaining Pirandello international recognition. His daughter Lietta marries Manuel Aguirre, Chilean military attaché, whom she met when he protected her during the riot after the première.

1922 Lord Chamberlain refuses permission for public production of *Six Characters in Search of an Author* in London, but private performance goes ahead in February. Production in New York in autumn. The critic Adriano Tilgher publishes a book containing essays which put Pirandello's theatre into a philosophic framework; the essay will not only condition the public's interpretation of Pirandello's work but will for a time influence Pirandello's self-view. In Milan, *Henry IV* staged, as is *To Clothe the Naked* in Rome. Several of his short stories adapted for the screen. Lietta, to the distress of her father, moves to Chile. Mussolini comes to power.

1923 *Six Characters in Search of an Author* staged to great acclaim in Paris in a version directed by Georges Pitoëff. Pirandello invited to many countries. Visits the USA in December for a season of his plays. *The Late Mattia Pascal* published in Britain and America.

*The Other Son*, *The Life I Gave You*, *The Man with the Flower in His Mouth* all premièred in Italy. Pirandello invited to meet Mussolini to discuss his impressions of America.

1924 Pirandello joins the Fascist party at the moment when Mussolini, following international condemnation of his involvement in the murder of the Socialist MP, Giacomo Matteotti, is at his weakest. *Each in His Own Way*, second part of the 'theatre-in-theatre' trilogy, produced in Milan. Father dies.

1925 Crucial year for Pirandello. Establishes in Rome own theatre company, Teatro d'Arte, with full government backing. The opening production is his own one-act piece, *Festival of Our Lord of the Ship*, which Mussolini attends. Pirandello embarks on a new career as director and producer; draws up a repertory of international theatre for the company. Undertakes tours in Britain, France, Germany, Austria, Czechoslovakia and Hungary. Meets the young actress, Marta Abba, who had been invited to join the troupe. The two form a deep, idiosyncratic and probably platonic relationship, intensely felt on Pirandello's side. She becomes his muse, his leading lady and the inspiration of the many plays he will write for her. Lietta returns from Chile with her husband, but finds that the father who had begged her to come back no longer wishes her in Italy. Returns to Chile.

1926 Financial problems for the new company; it relinquishes the initial hope of establishing a permanent base and becomes a touring venture. *Diana and Tuda*, influenced by Tilgher and starring Marta Abba, opens in German translation in Zurich. Pirandello's popularity in Italy on the wane, and increasingly his plays will be premièred abroad. Publication of *One, No One and One Hundred Thousand*, his last novel.

1927 Finally able to give up teaching. Tour of Brazil and Argentina. *The Wives' Friend*, whose protagonist is given the name 'Marta', premièred with Marta Abba in the leading role.

1928 Première of *The New Colony*, a work which Pirandello describes as a 'myth', final great success for the Teatro d'Arte, which breaks up. Marta Abba establishes her own company, dedicated principally to staging works by Pirandello. Pirandello leaves Italy and settles in Berlin.

1929 Elected member of the newly founded Accademia d'Italia by the Fascist government. Première of second 'myth', *Lazarus*, in English in Huddersfield. Subsequently staged in Rome with Marta Abba.

1930 Marta Abba takes the leading role in *As You Desire Me*, set partly in Germany. Later made into a Hollywood film with Greta Garbo and Erich von Stroheim. Première of *Tonight We Improvise*, final part of his 'theatre-in-theatre' trilogy, in German in Koenigsberg. Leaves Germany to return to Rome.

1931 *A Dream (But Perhaps Not)* premièred in Portuguese in Lisbon. Takes up writing short stories once again.

1932 *Finding Oneself* staged by Marta Abba's company in Naples.

1933 *When You Are Someone* staged first in Spanish in Buenos Aires, then by Marta Abba in Italy. Pirandello goes on lecture tour to South America and Scandinavia.

1934 *The Fable of the Changeling Son*, an opera with libretto by Pirandello and music by Gian Piero Malipiero, premièred in German in the presence of Hitler. The work was considered offensive to the German state. Mussolini walks out of the later Italian première. Awarded the Nobel Prize for literature. *You Don't Know How* produced in Czech in Prague.

1936 Falls ill with pneumonia while assisting at the filming of *The Late Mattia Pascal*. Dies at his house in Rome, leaving orders forbidding all state ceremonial and requesting that his body be cremated so that 'nothing at all will remain'. Ashes interred under a pine tree in Agrigento. Leaves unfinished his final 'myth', *The Mountain Giants*, premièred the following year in Florence.

# Plot

It is unusually difficult to give an accurate or helpful summary of *Six Characters in Search of an Author*, since it is of its nature a fragmentary piece, in which information on the central action is released fitfully and is accompanied by a semi-philosophical dialogue on the implications of what is occurring, often carried on by speakers who are unsure of the meaning of what they are witnessing. In addition, the structure is more complex not only than that of a conventional play but even of the play-within-a-play. There is an outer play and an inner play, but the relations between the two are delicate, and subject to change. Using the vocabulary Pirandello employs in his Preface, the outer play could be defined as 'philosophical' and the inner play involving the characters as 'historical'. The very terminology used to discuss this work requires care, since while all those who appear in a work of the imagination can normally be referred to as 'characters', in this case it is necessary to distinguish between 'characters' and human beings, even if both are, in another sense, fictional. There are different dimensions of action and of character in the play, with the categories of actor and character sharply divided. Madame Pace does not quite belong to either camp, while the Father and the Producer liaise between the two. Inside the category of character, the individuals depicted have, by the author's own admission, varying levels of dramatic realisation. This complexity is challenging but is appropriate for a multi-layered play which deals at one level with the nature of theatre, the mystery of imaginative creativity and the clashes between Life and Art, and at another with suffering humanity, the bitterness of family break-down, the pathology of guilt and the need for some reckoning for wrongs perpetrated and endured.

*Act One*

In the original Italian, there is no division into acts, but there are two breaks, corresponding to the moments when the Producer and the characters withdraw to sketch out the plot, and to when the stage-hand misunderstands instructions and pulls down the curtains.

The audience are given no precise national or city setting and no indication of the age in which the action occurs. Presumably the country is Italy, perhaps the city is Rome, probably the times are modern, but the dilemmas are transcendent and not dependent on historical, cultural or political factors. The work unfolds in a theatre, and occurs in the actual time in which the real spectators in the stalls watch the play. On entering, those spectators will see the chaos of a rehearsal room, not the meticulously designed production set. The actors enter randomly, not in costume, and stand around aimlessly until the Producer turns up and calls them to order. The play in rehearsal is Pirandello's own work *The Rules of the Game.*

The rehearsals are interrupted by one of the most celebrated entrances in modern drama. The stage doorkeeper walks up the aisle with several individuals, all members of the one family, who demand to see the Producer. There are six of them – the Father, the Mother, the Stepdaughter, the Son and a younger Boy and Girl who cling to the mother's skirts. These individuals are not of the same order of creation as the actors or of any other flesh-and-blood human beings. They are of their very essence *characters* who have been conceived by the imagination of some writer who has then decided not to write the drama in which they should have had their being. Pirandello insists that the difference in nature must be made apparent, perhaps by having them don masks, each expressing one fixed fundamental emotion, or by having them bathed in different coloured lights. To the Producer, indignant over having his rehearsals disrupted, they explain that having been abandoned by their own author they are in search of another. They carry in themselves a drama and offer the Producer the chance of presenting them as a new play.

Not all six characters are equally forthright. The Father, principally, and the Stepdaughter emerge as the group spokespersons with the Producer, and initially all are united in their quest for access to the stage or, in their terms, to that level of life which is theirs by right of birth as a character. Later that solid front will disintegrate as the drama itself unfolds and the divisions and rancour between the characters, especially the Father and the Stepdaughter, come to the fore. The two try to entice the Producer with the promise of success and wealth from their play, but they also ensnare him intellectually by inviting him to probe the essence of theatre. The Father shows himself to be a refined thinker and fluent speaker, who discourses on the nature of theatre and expounds to the cast the paradox that a character could be superior to a human being, because an invented being like Sancho Panza has the promise of eternity denied humankind. As the Producer becomes intrigued by the potential of the situation, the characters' solidarity begins to break down and the first outlines of their history begin to emerge. The Stepdaughter introduces the others, explaining that she and the two small children are illegitimate and for that reason the legitimate Son looks down on them.

We learn that the Mother and her three illegitimate children are in mourning for their recently deceased father, but that her deepest sadness is occasioned by the scorn with which she is treated by her eldest, legitimate son, born of the character known as the Father. At some stage in her past, the Mother had left the Father, her lawful husband, to go off with his secretary, but the reasons for this move are contested. The exposition of the facts of the case is complicated by the characters' individual efforts to set out their evaluation of what occurred. The Father requires to excuse and justify himself, while the Mother and the Stepdaughter, each in her own way, seek to reproach him for his conduct. His version is that he had noted a tenderness between the Mother and the secretary and had made it possible for them to set up home together. At the same time, he had dispatched the Son to some carer in the country who would ensure his well-being. The alternative view put forward by the Stepdaughter is that he was only interested in his own ease, and got rid of anyone who might interfere with it. After the separation, he continued to take an interest in his former family, even going to see the Stepdaughter as she went to school, but there is an implication that his motives were voyeuristic or even abusive. His presence upset the new couple, who moved town and left him no indication of their new whereabouts. All these details, the Father states, are only the indispensable information to make comprehensible the real drama, which starts at this point.

The Mother and her three children had returned to the town where they had previously lived, and where the Father is still resident, but at this point the contrasting interpretations offered by the individual characters become as crucial as the chronicle itself. The Producer demands that they get to the point but the Father insists that 'a fact is like a sack – it won't stand up if it's empty'. On the death of the ex-secretary, father of the Stepdaughter and of the two young children, the family are reduced to poverty, and the Mother is obliged to work as a seamstress for Madame Pace, whose real business is running a brothel and whose real intention is to have the Stepdaughter operate as a prostitute in her employ. The Father plainly has some as yet undivulged guilty secret, and intervenes to explain his predicament: he was still driven by sexual desire, was now too old to be attractive to women, was thus obliged to pay for sex and for that reason – explicable and justifiable in his eyes – became a client of Madame Pace's institution. The Father unburdens himself to anyone who will listen, proclaiming the injustice of his being judged on the basis of one moment of depravity while the rest of the time he is a man with solid aspirations to moral conduct; in Pirandellian terms, this view is converted to a complaint of having unjustly imposed on him a mask he does not deserve, that of a lascivious preyer on young women. The Stepdaughter will have none of this. Her impulse is to seek revenge for the humiliation to which he had subjected her and, in different ways, the whole family. She also reproaches the Son for the contempt with which he viewed the others when they moved back to the Father's house, where the Son had been the sole, privileged occupant. He in his turn claims to have been disconcerted by the arrival of this group of strangers, and particularly by the familiar conduct of this young, sensual woman towards his father, while she alleges that his problem was merely conceit over his legitimate birth versus their status as bastards.

Meantime, the outer story, of the encounter between the characters and the cast, especially the Producer, moves forward. The Producer is increasingly intrigued by the sinewy tale expounded to him, but is still puzzled by the people who are setting it out. To the disbelief and irritation of the actors, he agrees to explore the possibility of drawing up an outline plot with a view to staging the piece, and retires to his office with the six characters to put on paper the broad lines of the action.

*Act Two*

The second section opens with the confusion of stage-hands bustling about under the Producer's instructions to prepare a set for the re-enactment of the encounter scene in Madame Pace's back shop. The characters make occasional interjections on the need for complete accuracy, since for them the scene represents life and therefore mere approximation is not acceptable, but the Producer, who is fully in control, reminds them that this is only a first rehearsal. The characters are dismayed by the discovery that what is a lived scene for them is in the Producer's eyes only the provisional run-through of a fiction, and that his intention is to entrust the final product to his actors. The clash between the characters and the actors becomes a factor in the developing outer play, as the characters react with derision to the people who will play them on stage, while the actors respond with indignation to the protests of the characters and to their supposed lack of understanding of the dramatic art.

The obstacle to proceeding with the action is the absence of Madame Pace herself, but the Father insists that once the set of her shop is prepared and the conditions are right, she will make her appearance. And she does, inexplicably, mysteriously, suddenly, out of nowhere, greeted with black terror by the human beings but with calm normality by the characters. This moment smashes asunder all pretence of realism. Madame Pace is there because art requires her, and no considerations of imitation of reality apply. The action now gets under way. This encounter between Father and Stepdaughter in Madame Pace's shop is the decisive event in the lives of the characters, and from it stems the obsessive need felt by each of them to explain themselves and to torment each other. However, the unfolding events are interrupted by the comments of the actors, by the insistence of the characters that their personal interpretation be given due weight and by differences between Producer and characters over the importance accorded to what is theatre for him and life for them. The events as depicted by the characters are brutal and seedy. The Stepdaughter, reduced to earning a living as a prostitute with Madame Pace, is in mourning for her father, but the Father, who arrives as a client, attempts to ingratiate himself by offering to buy her a hat and, when she points to her mourning, suggests she remove her black dress. The departure from accepted notions of taste in the scene causes some alarm to the Producer, and he calls a halt to allow his actors to take over.

The characters are dismissive of the actors' efforts to imitate them, even if it is done in accordance with high actorial standards. Once again the clash between theatre and life takes precedence over the developing action, but only briefly. The rehearsal grinds to a halt as the Stepdaughter presses the Producer to allow the scene to proceed and to ignore the pleadings of the Father to be permitted to give priority to the claims of his conscience. She also calls on the Mother, in spite of her distaste for the whole business, to play her decisive role in what the Father calls the 'eternal moment'. It is the Stepdaughter who assumes command, getting the seduction scene under way, laying her head on the Father's chest, preparing to give herself to him and only the desperate scream of the Mother, who has realised at the last moment that it is her ex-husband who is about to have intercourse with her daughter, prevents the act of near-incest occurring. The Producer is overwhelmed by the dramatic strength of the scene, and transforms it in his mind to a grand climax. In his excitement, he marks the moment when the curtain would fall, but an ingenuous stage-hand takes this for an instruction, bringing this section to a close.

*Act Three*

The curtain rises to reveal further preparatory work on stage, this time on the set of the garden in the Father's house where, in the inner play, the six characters have taken up uneasy residence together. Since the abstract discussions and even the stage directions are integral to the unravelling of the total work, it is worth underlining that the directions indicate that the characters and actors will enter separately from opposite sides of the stage, and that the Producer will take his stance between them.

Before the second act of the characters' play can get under way, the Father and Producer are caught up in an acrimonious but paradoxical debate about the validity of the illusion offered by theatre actors as against the reality of the life lived by the invented characters, and about the superiority of characters (because of their 'eternal reality') over human beings. The being of characters is not subject to alteration, whereas for humans what seems reality today could appear tomorrow to be mere illusion. Does not the Producer, the Father wonders, in one of the fundamental questions put in the play, feel the earth give way under his feet when faced with this unsettling notion? Is not his idea of reality and his hold on it unstable and precarious? It is in part on account of this superiority that the characters feel so bitterly about the denial of life by their author, which left them in a limbo.

In the projected scene, the expectation is that the little children will be playing happily in a garden, so the stage is equipped with appropriate props. The Boy, who never speaks, is hidden behind a tree, while the Girl sits near a fountain. The remaining problem concerns the haughty Son, who refuses to participate and tries to make off, but forces stronger than himself pull him back, as the Stepdaughter has foretold. The author wished it that way, and their reality is not amenable to change. The characters now act, or live, their tragic scene, with the Producer and actors as onlookers.

The Stepdaughter has now assumed the directorial role, arranging the characters in their places and providing a commentary on the unfolding events. She reveals to the horrified spectators that the Boy, lingering near the fountain, has a revolver in his pocket. She leads the little Girl over to the fountain, inviting her to lie down. The Mother, prompted by the Stepdaughter, admits that she had gone to the Son's room to remonstrate with him over his loveless conduct towards her, but the Son refuses to take part in the re-enactment until the Father compels him. The Son and the Producer now argue over why he came to the theatre and his role in the scene, with the Son reluctantly stating that he left his room and ran down to the garden, followed by the Mother. There he found the Girl's body floating in the fountain, under the eyes of her brother who, if he had not actually killed her, had at least done nothing to prevent her death. At that point, on stage a shot rings out. The Boy has fired his revolver and killed himself. Is this an act of suicide carried out in reality on stage in the presence of the aghast actors and Producer, or is this an illusion of the sort that drama produces evening after evening? In the mêlée, voices are raised, shouting is heard from those who believe that it is reality and from those who believe it is only fiction. Nothing could be more totally Pirandellian.

It is the Producer who first comes to his senses and resumes control of himself and of the situation. He damns the lot of them for the lost rehearsal, tells the actors to take the rest of the day off and remains alone in the darkened and deserted theatre. In that obscurity, the shadows of four characters, minus the little Boy and Girl, appear in a mysterious, haunting half-light. All four, watched by the Producer alone, come together centre stage, the Mother still gesturing disconsolately towards her heartless Son before the Stepdaughter detaches herself from the others and runs down through the stalls, laughing hysterically and loudly. The three members of the original, legitimate family now reconstituted on the stage, are left alone as the curtain falls.

# Commentary

## The evolution from realism

Although he is, especially outside Italy, known principally as a playwright, Pirandello was in his forties when he came to theatre, and he came, surprisingly, encumbered with a baggage of hostility and distrust. In part, his animosity was aimed at the specific style of commercial or romantic drama then in vogue in Italy and Europe as a whole, but he had also a more deeply rooted suspicion of the very nature and practice of theatre. One eminent Italian critic, Paolo Puppa, has written that Pirandello had 'no love for the theatre',[1] and however unlikely that assessment may seem for a man who wrote so much for the stage, the judgement is well founded.

Pirandello had already tasted success in other genres of literature. His versatility was remarkable, as is apparent from the volumes of short stories, poetry, novels, essays and critical works he had produced. By the time of his theatrical debut in 1910 he had travelled a long way from the literary beliefs to which he had given allegiance in his youth. However much he wished to deny it later,[2] Pirandello's early writings were in line with a style of writing, particularly strong in Sicily, known as *verismo*, which may be regarded as the Italian variant of European realism or naturalism. He was always an unorthodox realist, but realism was scarcely a tightly bound school, and no one writer anywhere was a perfect, uncritical model of realism.

The term 'realism' has been used in a variety of different ways throughout the course of European history. In current

[1] Paolo Puppa, *Dalle parti di Pirandello* (Rome, Bulzoni, 1987), p. 23.
[2] See his interview with Domenico Vittorini in *High Points in the History of Italian Literature*, p. 256.

speech, it is almost a synonym for common sense, making it distinct from any other outlook which, however admirable in itself, would be considered too idealistic or utopian to be feasible. When applied to the literature of the past the term is used, loosely and anachronistically, to designate those writers who are ill-at-ease with any undue emphasis placed on fantasy, or who are considered to give an accurate depiction of conditions of life, particularly of the more brutal aspects of endurance against the odds. In this sense, Shakespeare could be said to give in his history plays a 'realistic' portrayal of warfare and battle, inasmuch as, far from repeating conventional slogans on martial glory and pride, he gives, through the character of Falstaff and the speech of the infantrymen, an account of the reality of fear, of the nature of pain and suffering from wounds, of the rejection by footsoldiers of grandiloquent notions of honour spoken by the captains and kings. Neither of these uses expresses what is meant by 'realism', or *verismo*, in its strict sense.

Space does not allow for a full treatment of this complex subject, but in summary it can be said that realism was a literary creed which emerged in Europe in the nineteenth century, in part as a reaction against Romanticism and in part as an expression of what can broadly be called the scientific spirit of the Victorian age. Romanticism in Britain is regarded as a literary movement which led William Wordsworth to address daffodils or Robert Burns to write poems on daisies and field-mice, and while it is true that Romanticism did involve a re-evaluation of nature, it was primarily a wider cultural movement, originating in Germany, which led to the assertion of the value of the individual, particularly of the grand, heroic individual. Works such as Goethe's *Young Werther*, or indeed Byron's *Manfred* or *Don Juan*, dealing with titanic, extraordinary individuals, are more authentic expressions of the Romantic spirit. In the Victorian age, on the other hand, there was an expectation and demand from the middle-class reader or theatre-goer to see himself and the dilemmas he faced in day-to-day life represented on stage or in the pages of fiction. Realism was, among other things, a response to that demand. Certainly the depiction of the bourgeoisie was not necessarily a respectful one, but in their desire to deal with everyday life and to depict recognisable social settings Dickens in Britain, Balzac in France, Dostoevsky in Russia and Galdos in Spain may be regarded as realists.

Realism developed its own ideology, and classic statements of it may be found in Zola's writings, especially his introduction to the stage version of *Thérèse Raquin* (1873) and his essay *Le Naturalisme au théâtre* (1878), or in the introduction written by the Swedish playwright August Strindberg to *Miss Julie* (1888). One of the dominant aspects of realism was the search for objective observation of social reality or of nature comparable to that provided by the scientist. The scientific method rather than science itself was the main object of the quest by realists, so the ideal model for the writer was not the imaginative creator of unseen worlds but the scientist with his microscope carefully recording his findings. Objective observation was the aim, and in order to attain that, the writer should strive to make himself invisible, since his own beliefs or prejudices were considered to be no more important than those of a scientist holding an implement. Writing of *Thérèse Raquin*, a story of adultery leading to murder, Zola said that he had 'simply applied to two living bodies the analytical methods surgeons apply to corpses'. The minds and psychology of human beings in society could, it was believed, be shown to operate and respond in determinable ways, as would their bodies when subjected to specific stimuli.

In Italy, realism was known as *verismo*, from *vero* which means 'true', and was particularly strong in Sicily. It was not restricted to the novel or theatre but made an impact on opera with works such as *Cavalleria rusticana*, which is also set in Sicily, and *I Pagliacci*. Giovanni Verga, Luigi Capuana and Federico De Roberto, all Sicilians, were the leading realist novelists and theorists of the new school, and all were deeply influenced by French thought and writings. It is Capuana who is given credit for introducing Pirandello to literary life in Rome around 1892, and pressing him to give up poetry and concentrate on prose and on depictions of his own time and his own people. Pirandello's first novel, *The Outcast Woman*, is a frank depiction of the plight of a Sicilian woman thrown out by her husband because she was accused, wrongly, of infidelity.

Many of his stories focus on moments, relaxed or tragic, of Sicilian experience, without any attempt to frame these experiences in a philosophical perspective. To use the distinction he was to employ in *Six Characters*, Pirandello was still a 'historical' rather than a 'philosophical' writer, but always his viewpoint was ironic and detached. 'The Jar', later adapted for the theatre, is a comic piece featuring a labourer who has invented a substance capable of mending fractured ceramics, and who is summoned by an avaricious farmer to repair a huge oil-jar which has been broken. Regrettably the labourer encloses himself in the jar while repairing it, and the peasants throw an improvised party, singing and dancing around him. He is inadvertently freed by the miserly farmer who is enraged at the din and knocks over his own jar. 'Ciaula Discovers the Moon' reflects directly the experience of many poor Sicilians around Agrigento, dealing as it does with a young man compelled to do night-shift in a sulphur mine, whose life is revolutionised when he is sent above ground and sees the moon for the first time. Other tales are more tragic. *The Other Son*, both as short story and play, could be taken as an example. An illiterate, poor woman uses a scribe to send letters to two sons who have gone off to the New World and totally abandoned her, but she shows no interest in the other son who has remained in Sicily and tries to look after her. It transpires that she cannot respond to this son because he was born of a rape when the woman had been kidnapped by a bandit, Cola Camizzi. There had been a bandit of that name, and he had tried on one occasion to murder Pirandello's father.

The bases of the realist view of art and creativity fell apart as it became clear that the parallels between the inventive imagination and the medical microscope were invalid and that all attempts to suppress the subjectivity of the author were doomed to failure. A portrait of a society given by an author in a work of fiction could never be objective. A curious example was given by the French author, Restif de la Bretonne, who set his novels in the seamier districts of Paris. His uncompromising portrayal of the lives of prostitutes, their clients and their environment won him many admirers until someone raised questions about the number of foot-fetishists that appeared in his fiction. Was this really a representation of the life of Parisians, or the private indulgence in an unusual taste which, it was discovered, the author himself enjoyed? Arnold Bennett, the only English writer who declared himself a realist in the sense the term was employed in continental Europe, noted in his *Journals* an oddity. He observed that in scenes of sexual encounters, the author would candidly and boldly describe female nudity, but would not feel the need to show the same candour over male nudity. How much did this evidently male urge show realism to be a sham, he wondered, never capable of moving beyond the personality of the (male) author?

The realist period passed, and Pirandello, like Strindberg, moved on. Looking back on his realist phase, he wrote:

> The realists limit art to the pure and simple imitation of nature: they do not claim to say anything: they want to represent nature as it is. It follows that the masterpiece of masterpieces will be the image given by a mirror. But why repeat with a lesser, human voice what nature says with its powerful voice? [. . .] Art is nature itself, but nature pursuing its work in the human spirit.[1]

The experience of realism left its mark, even when

[1] *Almanacco Letterario Bompiani, 1938*, reprinted as *Almanacco Bompiani, 1987*, ed. Leonardo Sciascia (Milan, Bompiani, 1986), p. 42.

Pirandello had turned his attention to the work of the 'human spirit'. He thought deeply about the nature of creativity, about the reality of characters and about the role of fantasy. Some trace of the impact of realism is to be found in *Six Characters* in the inner play, the play-within-a-play, in what the Father terms the 'painful drama' which the characters come to the theatre to represent. The attention of most audiences will go, as the analytic efforts of most critics always have, to certain themes: the interplay between the actors and the characters, questions of varying levels of life, the theory of theatre implicit in the dialogue between Father and Producer and the philosophy of life which emerges from the conflict. However, the story the characters themselves strive to tell, or live, is in keeping with the kind of plots featured in realist drama. In terms of the distinction Pirandello makes in the 1925 Preface to *Six Characters* (pp. 204–5) between 'historical' and 'philosophical', the category 'historical' is close to what was previously called 'realist'. The characters' rejected story is in many ways a 'realist' tale, but it comes wrapped in the 'philosophical' tale of their quest for life. The characters tell a tale of a dysfunctional family, a recurring theme of realist drama, whose behaviour clashes with the laws of secular and religious society. The family's own seething dissatisfaction with itself, its inability to contain in itself and express the needs of each of the individuals which constitute it, its clash with the ethics and mores of society, all contribute to its implosion and self-destruction. The Mother, little though she is allowed to speak, craves more attention or love; the Father leaves her for complex reasons which he subsequently, obsessively, needs to justify to himself; the children look on with various levels of disbelief, haughty disdain or angry reproach. The Father is moved by sexual urges which he himself judges shameful but which he cannot deny and which bring him to the point of actual, if unintentional, incest. In other words, the issues sketched out in the few scenes the characters are permitted to perform include the most basic of human appetites and the most universal of taboos – adultery, illegitimacy, incest, family violence, murder and suicide. Pirandello drew back from his own invention. He states in his Preface that he decided not to write that play. 'It is very true,' he writes, 'I did not at all represent that drama: I presented another' (p. 215). His refusal was futile, since in the drama the characters did manage to stage the outlines of the dreadful events which befell them became clear.

Pirandello had moved far beyond the parameters of realism, and had given himself a liberty of artistic inventiveness which realism would have denied. G. K. Chesterton once wrote that Victorian fantasy stories, whether fairy tales or ghost stories, were the reverse side of the cult of realism. Pirandello used fantasy in ways which were anything but playful or fit for children's stories to express dilemmas and beliefs which had the seriousness of philosophy. The characters who, he insists in the stage directions, must be distinguished from their first entrance from human beings, are as much creatures of fantasy as Peter Pan and the children of Never-Never-Land, but they are bereft of all trace of innocence. An even more sharp break with realism is given by the appearance of Madame Pace, whose appearance is subject to no rules of plausibility or credibility. She comes to life because the story requires her. Her existence is purely a function of the tormented story of the Father and Stepdaughter, but she is no phantasm or other-worldly creature, unless that other-world is the realm of art. She has the earthiness of an unscrupulous, unlovely and exploitative criminal who could have appeared in a hundred realist novels, but her appearance here smashes every detail of the realist creed.

However far he had travelled by the time of the 1921 première of *Six Characters*, Pirandello made his way to and in theatre with the support of the realists. It has already been pointed out that Pirandello owed his introduction to the world of letters to Luigi Capuana, a Sicilian and a theorist of realism; he owed his introduction to theatre to two other Sicilians, both experienced theatre men. In 1910,

Nino Martoglio, actor-author from Catania, encouraged Pirandello to write a script. Adopting a practice which was to become common with him, Pirandello adapted two short stories, 'The Vice' and 'The Epilogue'. These works were relatively successful, but he had less fortune in 1915 when the meaning of another play *If Not Thus* was completely twisted by the company who staged it, especially by its leading actress, Irma Gramatica. In a letter that year, Pirandello stated his intention of giving up writing for the theatre. He relented when Martoglio encouraged him to offer something to Angelo Musco, a Sicilian actor-manager then at the height of his popularity. Pirandello's scripts for Musco were not in Italian but in Sicilian dialect, and all were well received.

This growing popularity did not lessen Pirandello's intellectual dissatisfaction with theatre. There were two aspects to this dissatisfaction. At one level, he was concerned about the role of the writer in Italian theatre as it was at the end of the nineteenth and the opening of the twentieth century. The prevailing culture of Italian theatre has always been distinctive. Its main difference from other European theatres lies in the fact that from its very origins with *commedia dell'arte* (which should be translated as 'professional theatre', since *arte* means 'guild' not 'art') the central figure of Italian theatre has been not the writer but the actor. In that tradition, nineteenth-century touring companies, such as Musco's own, preferred to work by improvisation on agreed storylines rather than learning and staging a writer's script. There is an anecdote that after a quarrel Pirandello threatened to take away his play, but was disconcerted to hear Musco retort that he had no more use of it since his players could improvise on a plot which was by now familiar to them. The centrality of the actor was more marked than ever in the nineteenth century with the rise to prominence of a generation of the 'great actor' – known to history immodestly as the *grande attore* – and later as the *mattatore*, a word whose origin is disputed but which may be a pun on the Spanish 'matador'. The great actor gathered around him a more or less permanent company of performers who were not permitted to challenge the supremacy of the charismatic leading figure. A performance was an opportunity for him or her (there were some actresses in this category) to show their abilities; actors or scriptwriters had to bear in mind that this was the prime requirement. This practice did not endear itself to Pirandello, who, being a writer, is something of an outsider to the central Italian tradition of theatre, although that is not to say that he was the only playwright the country has produced.

In Pirandello's lifetime, a wholly new figure, that of the director, began to emerge. It was only in the late nineteenth century that the need for the co-ordinating skills of the director began to make itself felt, firstly in Germany, later in France and last of all in Italy. There was not even a settled Italian term for this figure, and in the plays which make up his theatre-in-theatre trilogy – *Each in His Own Way* (1924) and *Tonight We Improvise* (1930) being the others – he uses different nouns for the figure. This distinction is lost in English translation, but the term *capocomico* used in *Six Characters* is the historical term used from the days of *commedia dell'arte*. In both these plays, the director is the object of satirical jibes by Pirandello, although this is more unremittingly so of Doctor Hinkfuss of *Each in His Own Way*. It is Pirandello himself who draws attention to the satirical elements towards contemporary theatre in *Six Characters*. He has, obviously, little respect for a theatre which believes that real drama is written in France. The criticism of the timidity of Italian theatre is too evident to need labouring, but in his Preface, Pirandello states roundly that:

> there is indeed a discreet satire of Romantic procedures; in those characters of mine, so heatedly overdoing things in the role each has in a certain drama while I present them as characters of another play which they do not know and do not suspect, so that their passionate agitation, common in Romantic proceedings, is humorously portrayed but leads nowhere. (p. 215)

There was, however, an altogether more profound aspect to Pirandello's anxieties over theatre. His difficulty lay in the very point which makes theatre distinct from other forms of literature, which makes it indeed a bastard form suspended half-way between writing and a performance art. Theatre is of its essence a collaborative genre, which requires the input of a writer but also of actors, of lighting engineers, sound designers, a director, stage manager and others. In some views, the writer is no more than *primus inter pares*. Pirandello resented this demotion of the writer as strongly as he disapproved of the downplaying of the writer in favour of the actor. In the essay 'Illustrators, Actors and Translators' (1908),[1] he expressed reservations about all these activities. The book illustrator is an unnecessary and damaging trespasser between the productive imagination of the writer and the receptive facilities of the reader, the translator is a vandal who cannot respect the 'specific feeling and even the graphic form of the words' of a language. The actor is the third in this series of figures who may be necessary, but whose presence is unwelcome:

> Unfortunately, there always has to be a third, unavoidable element that intrudes between the dramatic author and the creation in the material being of the performance: the actor.
>
> As is well known, this is an unavoidable limitation for dramatic art. Just as the author has to merge with his character in order to make it live, to the point of feeling as it feels, desiring as it desires itself, so also to no lesser degree, if that can be accomplished, must the actor.
>
> But even when one finds a great actor who can strip himself completely of his own individuality and enter into that of the character that he is playing, a total, full incarnation is often hindered by unavoidable facts, by the actor's appearance, for example [. . .]
>
> And that same distasteful surprise we feel when we read an illustrated book, and see in the illustrator's portrayal a picture quite different from the one we had imagined of a person or a

[1] Reprinted in Basnett and Lorch, pp. 23–34.

> scene, is felt by the dramatic author when he sees his own play acted out by actors in a theatre [. . .]
>
> Now what does an actor do? He does exactly the opposite of what the writer does. That is, he makes more real yet less true that character created by the writer, he takes away from him just so much ideal, superior truth as he gives back in ordinary, material reality, and makes him less true because he is translating him into the fictitious, conventional reality of the stage. (Basnett and Lorch, pp. 27–9)

Pirandello later revised his views when, with the foundation of the Teatro d'Arte, he became producer and director and worked in close collaboration with his cast. With this company, he directed the second version of *Six Characters* in 1925, but the views of actors in this play are a throwback to his earlier opinions of the profession. While there are in *Six Characters* deeper strands to his thinking, the meditation on the nature of artistic creation, the views on Romantic drama, on realism and on acting all contribute to its enigmatic, ambiguous richness.

## The poetics of Pirandellism

There is a special class of writer whose importance can be measured by the fact that he has given the world not only a body of work but also an adjective to describe particular habits of mind, moral dilemmas or existential enigmas recognised by their contemporaries but perhaps unknown to them until the diagnosis or description was made public. Franz Kafka's name has provided the adjective 'Kafkaesque' to indicate the plight of individuals caught up in a threatening bureaucratic mire beyond their comprehension, while 'Borgesian', from the Argentinian J. L. Borges, is now the label attached to a mind and imagination lost in a labyrinthine situation where truth and fantasy overlap. From the name Pirandello, at least in Italian, both an adjective and a noun have been forged to express a complex of ideas first articulated in the writer's work on multiple personality, truth and doubt, life and form, reality and appearance.

Pirandello is not a writer whose work is concerned exclusively with emotions – although his plays do feature characters caught up in tragic emotional entanglements – nor with narrow social conflicts. His characters tend to approach their emotional problems through intellectual anxiety, or show an ability to convert intellectual dilemmas into raw passion. Pirandello's theatre can only be fully appreciated once the body of ideas identified as '*Pirandellismo*' which his theatre contains, expounds and debates is grasped. There are two extremes to be avoided: the older tendency to dissect the plays exclusively in the sub-philosophical terms of *Pirandellismo*, and the more recent, opposing tendency to approach the plays without regard for ideas. Pirandello's theatre is rich and challenging on both the intellectual and emotional level, and perhaps it might be helpful to see in him two souls, even if the separation will never be complete: the 'humorist' Pirandello and the *Pirandellist* Pirandello.

*Pirandellismo* is a complex phenomenon, with depths and ambiguities which it is not possible to debate here. One concerns the roots of Pirandello's notions. He was Sicilian by birth, education and culture, but spent a significant portion of his formative years in Germany at a time when the great nineteenth-century tradition of German philosophy, the school of thought known to history as Idealism, was coming to an end. Different critics have given varying weight to the impact of these two facts. The Marxist thinker, Antonio Gramsci, and the Sicilian writer, Leonardo Sciascia, both believed that Pirandellism was a sophisticated expression of Sicilian popular culture, and that the search for origins of notions of multiple personality and of clashes between reality and appearance should be conducted as in archaeology: the deepest layer would reveal traces of a Mediterranean society where a code of honour, especially in sexual morals, imposed rigid, often deadly requirements that could be avoided only by a practice of systematic concealment, and only the more recent, upper layers would expose deposits from disparate, perhaps largely German, sources. Sciascia believed that the coining of the term Pirandellism had simply muddied the waters, and preferred to denote it a 'half-philosophy' rather than a philosophy. In this view, Pirandello's outlook was the sum of his poetic responses to, and reflections on, the experiences, sufferings (many) and joys (few) of his characters. On the other hand, the Anglo-American critic Eric Bentley believed that in his theatre Pirandello had made a 'personal digest of nineteenth-century German philosophy' (Bentley, 1972, p. 24).

Pirandello gave support at various times both to those who detected some form of semi-philosophy and to those who held that the drama he offered and the response he asked of his audiences were no different from that sought by a less intellectual author. Perhaps the distinction is unimportant. Theatre at its best is a forum for the discussion and testing of ideas as well as of exploring emotions, and Pirandello concerned himself with the ordinary dramatic business of finding in successive plays the means of holding the attention of the audience while examining ideas. A play can only be about the things that the characters are plausibly interested in, or in the implications of their individual dilemmas, whether or not these can be called 'philosophical'. In his Preface to *Six Characters*, he wrote that the characters embodied 'the passion and torment which for so many years have been the passion and torment of my spirit', but later in the same Preface, he added that it would be a mistake to view the play as an artificially preconceived device to give abstract convictions dramatic form:

> The fact is the play was really conceived in one of those spontaneous illuminations of the fantasy when by a miracle all the elements of the mind answer to each other's call and work in divine accord. No human brain, working 'in the cold', however stirred up it might be, could ever have succeeded in penetrating far enough, could ever have been in a position to

> satisfy all the exigencies of the play's form. Therefore, the reasons I will give to clarify the values of the play must not be thought of as intentions I conceived beforehand [. . .] but only as discoveries I have been able to make afterwards in tranquillity. (p. 209)

Another complexity relating to the presence or absence of a philosophy in Pirandello concerns the influence of the critic Adriano Tilgher. The relations between the two, complicated by the fact that Pirandello joined the Fascist party while Tilgher remained one of Fascism's staunchest opponents, are unique in the history of literature, in that the critic Tilgher modified and enhanced, rather than merely followed and commented on, the development of the writer Pirandello. Once again there are disputes over the degree of influence, and there are those whose ideal is to present a Pirandello cleansed of Tilgher, but Pirandello himself acknowledged Tilgher's contribution in at least clarifying his thinking and providing him with a vocabulary to debate 'the passion and torment' which lay at the heart of his theatre. Tilgher wrote a largely critical review of *Six Characters* after its 1921 première, and the following year published a book containing an essay in which he said that the very essence of Pirandello's theatre lay in the clash it dramatised between Life and Form. In this view, Life was conceived as an anarchic, shapeless, unintelligible flow which was arrested, moulded and given manageable outlines by a static force denominated Form. Form was thus both a distortion of Life, since Life in itself was unknowable and uncontrollable, and a necessity for human beings who could not cope with Life without the superimposition of Form. Pirandello's theatre was, in Tilgher's view, a dialectic art form, a dramatisation of the clash between these two powers in permanent conflict. Tilgher was himself a student of German philosophy, and the notion of the centrality of the dialectical process originated in the philosophies of Hegel and Marx. Pirandello initially responded warmly to this interpretation, with the mild objection that the intellectual framework

Tilgher advanced had been part of his thinking before the appearance of the critic's essays. Pirandello had himself studied in Germany, and it is true that a letter to his son Stefano in 1917 when the latter was a prisoner-of-war contained the warning:

> There are in you, my son, many possibilities of being. To give them a form will not be easy for you. You will regrettably have to adapt to one which does not involve the irremediable sacrifice of all the others: one which is capable of some development and which can harmoniously contain the totality of your being while also according with the necessities of your life. This is a thorny problem. The unhappiness of many people arises in large part from not having been able to resolve it.[1]

However, the Life/Form antithesis was incorporated more strongly and frequently into his own essays and theatre after the publication of Tilgher's book. The most obvious dramatisation of this clash was the play *Diana and the Tuda*, premièred in Germany in 1926. The work features two sculptors, one of whom attempts to give mythological form to the life-force who is Tuda, and although it is a limp, unconvincing work, the Life–Form clash lies at its heart. It is a central constituent of *Pirandellismo* and appears in *Six Characters*.

The idea was as unconventional then as now, but Pirandello had no hesitation over shocking the audience into facing situations they would have preferred to shun or challenging them to question everyday beliefs. In a letter to the director of one of his most successful and frequently performed pieces, *Right You Are! (If You Think So)*,[2] he wrote:

[1] *Almanacco Letterario Bompiani, 1938*, p. 42, republished as appendix to *Almanacco Bompiani, 1987*, ed. Leonardo Sciascia (Milan, Bompiani, 1986).

[2] For its most recent production in London in 2003, directed by Franco Zeffirelli, the title was translated by Martin Sherman as *Absolutely! (Perhaps)* (London, Methuen, 2003).

> The Public? For my part, I have made my public expect of me all kinds of outrageous things. I have gone out of my way to offend my public and the public knows it [. . .] All my work has always been and will always be like that: a challenge to the opinions of the public and above all to its moral – or immoral – peace.[1]

In the same correspondence, he described *Right You Are!* as being 'based in a strange and unusual way on the validity of reality'. This notion too is intrinsic to Pirandellism. It is a vast and overwhelming theme, and remains so if Pirandello's swaggering assertion is rewritten to make it a challenge to 'received ideas about the validity of truth'. Pirandello's theatre tackles deep, fundamental questions of life and knowledge, and he requires a seriousness of response equal to the seriousness and breadth of his intentions. In *Right You Are! (If You Think So)* he tantalises spectators with the question of how much of truth is knowable, and of how much truth humanity can cope with. The setting is an ordinary, well-to-do house in some unidentified location. In spite of the impression given by *Six Characters*, Pirandello rarely experiments with dramatic structure or form. Like G. B. Shaw, he prefers to use traditional settings, but then overturns expectations by the disturbing, unsettling nature of what is said in these drawing rooms and well-kept gardens. The enigma facing the townsfolk concerns the odd conduct of a newly arrived family consisting of a married couple and the wife's mother, but with the oddity that the husband refuses to allow the mother access to her daughter. Pirandello brings on stage one after the other Signora Frola, the mother, who explains that she loves her son-in-law, Signor Ponza, and respects his obsessive jealousy, then the son-in-law who claims that Signora Frola went mad when her real daughter, his first wife, was killed in an earthquake and that the explanation of his seemingly oppressive behaviour is that she has come to believe that his second wife is her

[1] Letter to Virginio Talli, quoted in Basnett and Lorch, p. 46.

daughter. No sooner have the townsfolk digested these contradictory revelations when the signora re-enters to provide a third explanation, that the madman is her son-in-law, driven insane by a lengthy separation from his wife and unable to recognise her when they were reunited.

The townspeople, enraged at their inability to reach any rational conclusion, are left floundering. What is clear is that the inner triangle of mother, son-in-law and wife are respositories of some secret suffering which they have resolved in their own way. There are three levels of character – the gossiping townspeople, the inner threesome, and the character of Laudisi, the *raisonneur*, who has the function of chorus or authorial spokesperson. Each scene ends with Laudisi's derisive laughter at the earnest, self-deluding quest of his neighbours for some absolute truth, but it is he who suggests that they solve the riddle by summoning the mysterious wife-daughter herself. This is of little value. She enters covered in a veil to say that she is both the daughter of Signora Frola and the second wife of Signor Ponza, and for herself 'no one. I am who I am believed to be', she announces to the dismay of her listeners and the delight of Laudisi.

The work is open to a range of not necessarily incompatible interpretations. It can be a re-affirmation of the plea made by Laudisi for tolerance of other people's views and privacy irrespective of how bizarre or contradictory these views seem, but it is also a powerful statement of the impossibility of ever attaining truth. This conviction that no absolute truth is knowable is another element of Pirandellism, and is restated in *Six Characters*. There may be truths, half-truths, well-founded opinions but there are no means given to human beings to distinguish confidently between truth and falsehood. Men and women have to content themselves with approximations, however paradoxical the formulations may be, as is that provided by the veiled lady in *Right You Are!*.

The play, as Pirandello promised, enrages those who expect a well-rounded, if not necessarily happy, ending, but such an ending would be incompatible with the beliefs, or half-philosophy, Pirandello was advancing. In the Pirandellian world-view, truth did not exist, so no question could be wholly resolved. The dénouement which traditional theatre offered is out of place. In different terms, the unmasking, the revelation of who's who, the removal of disguise to reveal the real nature of identity, was impossible in Pirandello. This point can be clarified by comparison with a play, Shakespeare's *Twelfth Night*, which has otherwise nothing whatsoever to do with Pirandello (although those with a taste for strange coincidence can ponder the fact that the Shakespearean play is subtitled *As You Will*). In Shakespeare, Viola dresses as a man to act as ambassador for her master, Orsino, to the Lady Olivia with whom he has fallen in love. The complication is that Viola herself falls in love with her master, while Olivia, believing the envoy is male, falls in love with her. The final twist is that Viola has a male twin, Sebastian, who turns up after escaping a shipwreck, and whose presence and gender permit a rounded dénouement and happy ending. Orsino and Viola, and Olivia and Sebastian are wed. The masks, in other words, are pulled off, the disguise revealed, the truth of identity established.

In Pirandello, the mask can never be pulled off and no truth can ever be established, because the system of belief in truth and personality which underlie Shakespeare is at odds with the system of ideas to which the mature Pirandello gave allegiance. The rules of the game are different. He rejects the standard belief that truth and falsehood can be differentiated and that mistakes in perception can be traced, identified and corrected. There is no reality beyond perception. The veiled woman of *Right You Are!* has no fixed, underlying identity only temporarily concealed by disguise or mask. Her statement that she is 'who she is believed to be' may be paradoxical and offensive to common sense, but it is an assertion of a new view of personality and of truth. In Pirandello, the personality of human beings is not fixed, unlike that of fictional characters. Personality is not one, but multiple, as the Father in *Six Characters* will endlessly proclaim. The veiled woman can be two contrasting things for two separate people – her mother and husband – and no principle of logic gainsays her right to view herself in such terms. Humans are more complex than they were believed to have been in traditional schemes of thought. Pirandello's final novel was given the title *One, No One and One Hundred Thousand* to denote the multiple possibilities of personality which exist in every one of us, and each of these masks has equal worth and claim to be viewed as 'true'.

This process of donning masks, and creating, however arbitrarily, some inner being is known in Pirandellian terminology as *costruirsi*, literally 'constructing oneself'. Nothing is given at birth or by virtue of humanity; there is no fixed selfhood which can be identified as the irreducible quintessence of an individual. In the absence of any such spiritual entity, human beings have no option but to engage in a process of erecting patterns of being, or roles in life, for themselves. 'Marriage, fatherhood, motherhood, and personality have no meaning except that which we give to them,'[1] he declared to Domenico Vittorini, the Italo-American author of a study of his theatre published in his lifetime. A human being cannot just *be*: he or she must act out a part. In that sense, not only is the being of theatrical characters superior to that of humans because it is beyond the realm of change or decay, but the theatre also provides the basic and truest metaphor for life. All the world is indeed a stage in a more all-encompassing sense than Shakespeare ever conceived, and on that stage human beings play their parts and wear their masks. Having rejected the centuries-old idea of one, stable, knowable identity or personality, Pirandello saw human beings as endowed not with a single personality but with multiple personalities. This may mean something simple and straightforward, that one man will be, in various spheres,

[1] Vittorini, 1958, p. 257.

son, husband, father, butcher, Christian, socialist, aviation expert, football enthusiast, patriot and the like, but in a deeper sphere it means that his psychic state, his self-image and social standing are similarly the result of the same process of self-construction. The goodness or wickedness of the mask thus donned, or the personality thus constructed, does not alter the fact that all personalities are constructed. The occasional recognition of this fact, normally only at moments of trauma, leads to insuperable crisis.

The deepest of all clashes in Pirandello's theatre is the clash between 'mask and face', present in both *Right You Are! (If You Think So)* and *Six Characters*. It is not even as simple as stating that behind an inauthentic mask there lies an authentic face, since in all likelihood behind one inauthentic mask lies another, or several, all equally authentic or inauthentic. Nevertheless, human beings, in Pirandello's view, are fated to engage in a struggle or extended protest against the restrictions or distortions the mask represents, since it is a reduction of their multiplicity and conceivably a distortion of their own self-view. Pirandello gave Vittorini his own definition of personality and the mask:

> The last generation looked upon nature and man as something existing in unchanging, clear-cut and solid forms outside of us. To me reality is something that we mould through the power of our imagination. I have given a quixotic treatment of this concept, especially in *Right You Are! (If You Think So)*, but the idea is fundamental to my art and it enlivens most of my works [. . .] We say, I am one, and we look upon our fellow men as solid, clear-cut personalities, while in reality we are the juxtaposition of infinite, blurred selves. We are multiple personalities. (Vittorini, 1958, p. 260)

In a profound sense, 'masks' shape the very being of the human creature, but not of the created character in drama or fiction, who will remain as he or she was invented. The encounter between the mysterious six characters and the cast of actors in *Six Characters* illuminates the nature both of theatre and of human life. The very terminology of 'mask' is itself theatrical, and a reproduction of jargon employed in Italian *commedia dell'arte* tradition. In it, the actors played parts which were recognisable to the public by the actual masks they wore, Harlequin with his lozenged costume and black mask with long, beaky nose being the best known, although there were many others. Their mask was their character, at least as far as the public were aware, and they were not amenable to the development which was seen in, for example, Shakespearean characters.

For Pirandello, human beings too wore masks, metaphorical masks, but they had also an inner life and any contrast between the outer mask and the inner self-awareness could be a cause of suffering. Reduced to its barest bones, this is the tragic dilemma facing the Father in *Six Characters*. A mask which he believes inappropriate has been imposed on him by his Stepdaughter, and his struggle – a struggle which by its very nature he cannot win – is to free himself of it and to don the mask he feels appropriate, that is, to assert himself in the terms he sees himself. The focus of Pirandello's later theatre is on the nature and personality of the individual human being, who he or she is, how they see themselves, how they are seen, how they cope with the gaps between these two acts of perception and how they might grapple with a hurtful view of themselves as held by others. In these terms, the clash is more familiar and human than might appear in the more abstract formulations of Pirandellism. 'The Whistle of the Train' features a man who becomes aware of the drudgery of the life he has lived day after day by simply hearing the whistle of a train as it roars through his town towards destinations he dreams about. He has heard the same sound from the same train on the same line countless times before, but on this occasion it shatters the compromise which is his life. Another character is brought to a comparable epiphany by seeing, as he had done every day, the nameplate on his door. The protagonist of the final novel, *One, No One and One Hundred Thousand*, is forced to confront his own mask after hearing a chance remark by his wife that his nose hangs to the right. It always had and he had never cared, but this statement has devastating results, leading him to lobby obsessively strangers and friends to establish whether this was the 'mask' he had always worn. If human beings are subject to this multiplicity, it could be said that invented, fictional characters belong, paradoxically, to a superior order of life, since Sancho Panza, Hamlet or Orestes have that stability, fixedness and unity of personality denied to creatures of flesh and blood. The Father in *Six Characters* relishes forcing his human hearers to face this seeming contradiction which is so demeaning for their sense of their own worth.

Pirandello gave such notions their most coherent expression in the Preface he wrote for *Six Characters*. The Preface appeared only when the 1925 edition was published, when he had had time to consider the contributions made by directors of the various productions in Italy and abroad and to ponder the validity of the reviews of his play. It is, in other words, a *post-factum* justification rather than a starting point. If it is also a rebuttal of criticisms, it provides a statement of his philosophical outlook. It should in justice be added that in the view of one recent critic the Preface is designed to put people off the track of the deep meaning of the play rather than aid enlightenment,[1] but this is a minority view.

The Preface has the drama of a short story, retracing the events outlined in the earlier tale, 'Tragedy of a Character'. He tells of the arrival, unbidden, of six characters with a harrowing story which they wish to live, and of their dismay at his decision as author to deny them that life to which as characters they have a claim. The reasons for Pirandello's rejection of them are based on the way he sees himself as a writer (on his own mask as writer). The fundamental distinction he makes is between two categories

[1] Andrea Camilleri, *Biografia del figlio cambiato* (Milan, Mondadori, 2001), p. 222.

of writer, 'historical' and 'philosophical'. Historical writers are broadly storytellers, who tell a tale for the sheer delight of telling it and who ask no more of a reader than that they engross themselves in the characterisation, setting, action and unfolding events of that one plot. Pirandello, however, belongs to the 'philosophical category', that is, he stands with those writers who 'feel a more profound spiritual need' and who will only relate characters, events, affairs which have been 'soaked, so to speak, in a particular sense of life and acquire from it a universal value' (p. 206). The term 'philosophical' can be misleading, since Pirandello emphasises that he has no sympathy for symbolism or allegory, where the unfolding storyline relies on an image deliberately devised to point to a moral or to illustrate a previously held conviction. Orwell's *Animal Farm*, for example, would have drawn Pirandello's strictures on this score. In Pirandello's view, philosophical writing should 'seek in an image, which must remain alive and free throughout, a meaning to give it value'. The 'freedom and life' are vital, and he wrote later in the same Preface that 'nothing in this play exists as given and preconceived. Everything is in the making' (p. 215). Crucially for him, he could not detect meaning in the story of the six characters. The plight they presented to him seemed to him no more than a dramatic tale, fit as such for 'historical' writers, perhaps even appealing to realist writers, but not to post-realist or 'philosophical' Pirandello. For that reason, he left the story unwritten, and denied the characters the level of life which was their due.

However, the relations between life and the stage, and the nature of artistic creation were other phenomena which intrigued Pirandello and since the characters continued to haunt his imagination, he hit on the device of allowing them to continue with 'this struggle for existence they have had with me' in a totally new kind of play. 'The result was what it had to be: a mixture of tragic and comic, fantastic and realistic, in a humorous situation which was quite new and infinitely complex' (p. 207). The language employed by

Pirandello in this passage draws attention to the multi-layered complexity of the plot. The fantasy – and in the opening passage of the Preface he had, as in the short story 'Tragedy of a Character', personified Fantasy as his housemaid – of the arrival of the characters in a theatre is overlaid on the realist tale they long to tell, while the word 'humorous' has that typically Pirandellian dual sense of arousing compassion as well as of causing that reluctant laughter which has to be stifled as inappropriate. From this new clash between creatures of fantasy and flesh-and-blood beings, from the internal conflict arising from the rage of character against character, and from their joint alliance against the Producer to wrest from him that licence they crave to live out their drama and their life, there finally emerges 'that universal meaning at first vainly sought in the six characters' (p. 208). If their own story of separation, family splits and sexual desire was limited and specific to those six characters alone, the plight of creatures seeking life and an understanding of the human condition gains that universality that Pirandello required as a pre-condition for writing. As the critic Siro Ferrone wrote, 'without an understanding of this basic obsession (death, eternity), the work of Pirandello is unintelligible.'[1] To talk of the quest for truth in theatre, to identify a theatre which seeks meaning in life and aims to be an instrument for pondering death and mortality is to risk falling into pompousness and facility, but Pirandello deserves the respect due to those few modern writers who have the ambition to grapple with themes of that universality and scope.

There is one further 'pang of the spirit', both personal to him and universal to humanity, which the six characters incarnate, 'the deceit of mutual understanding, irremediably founded on the empty abstraction of words' (p. 208). The 'problem of communication' was to haunt writers throughout the twentieth century, making unlikely

[1] Siro Ferrone, intro. to *Sei personaggi in cerca d'autore* (Milan, Rizzoli, 1993), p. 11.

bedfellows of such adversaries as T. S. Eliot and Jean-Paul Sartre, but it was Pirandello who first made the problem central to his drama. Human communication, the free exchange of ideas and emotions, is not the simple transaction it might appear, but a process vitiated by the very currency of that exchange, words. Identical words indicating seemingly similar concepts – love, hate, fear, desire – are false friends since the speaker and the listener will refer them not to some common store of human feelings but to the individual experience of each individual soul. The uniqueness of the memories of these experiences militates against communicability. The recollection and the reaction of the Father and the Stepdaughter to the shared moment of their lives in the brothel run by Madame Pace are incompatible the one with the other, both on a human and Pirandellist level.

Pirandellism is both a semi-philosophy and a theory of drama. It is both a complex of deeply held ideas on life and a series of intuitions and reflections on experience. As much on account of this combination as for its enigmatic pondering of human and fictional life, *Six Characters in Search of an Author* has been defined by Peter Szondi as 'the quintessence of modern drama'.[1]

## Humour, cruelty and compassion

There will be to readers of Pirandello's novels or plays, familiar with the bleakness of vision which emerges so forcibly in them, something paradoxical if not perverse in the description of him as a 'humorist', but it was a definition which, unlike others applied to him by critics, he chose for himself. Pirandello was not an author whose writing was guided or shaped by instinct or unexamined ideas in the air at the time, but a deeply introspective, reflective writer who thought about his craft, and who expressed in his creative work the outlook – he was chary

[1] Quoted by Camilleri, op. cit., p. 221.

of the use of the word 'philosophy' – he expounded in depth in a number of theoretical, abstract works. The categories of essay, short story, novel, drama or poetry cannot be kept apart. One critic spoke of an 'intercommunicability' between the various genres of Pirandello's writing. 'It is like a vast terrain on which continuous irrigation canals run: the imaginative lands are nourished by remarks, philosophical considerations, polemical thoughts, insistent themes and "concepts" which bounce like elastic balls from one work to the next, often in the same words.'[1]

Two theoretical works are indispensable to the appreciation of Pirandello's literary output, fiction as well as drama: The Preface to *Six Characters*, which we have already considered, and the essay 'On Humour' (*L'Umorismo*), published in 1908,[2] a meditation on his distinctive outlook on life and writing. The essay is divided into two sections, the first a historical-critical survey of writers who can be viewed as 'humorists', and the second an exposition of Pirandello's own views. His understanding of the term is idiosyncratic and highly personal. 'We must not confuse real *umorismo* with English *humour* [English word used in the original], that is, with that typical way of laughing or mood which, like every other people in the world, the English too have' (p. 115). Humour is not the buffoonery of farce or the drollery of, say, P. G. Wodehouse. It has nothing in common with the terms with which it is normally taken as synonymous, or at least closely compatible. It is not dependent on burlesque, ridicule, wit, grotesque, facetiousness, nor is it even a technique necessarily designed to arouse laughter. In his own creative writing, Pirandello

[1] Giovanni Macchia, *Storia della letteratura italiana*, volume IX (Milan, Garzanti, 1969), p. 444.

[2] Both essays are included in Luigi Pirandello, *Saggi e scritti vari*, ed. Manlio Lo Vecchio-Musti (Milan, Mondadori, 1960). All page references to the essay 'On Humour' (*L'Umorismo*) are to the Italian edition, intro. Salvatore Gugliemino (Milan, Mondadori, 1992); translation J. Farrell.

has little taste for whimsy, rarely shows any light wit, and has no interest in a display of an offhand talent to amuse. There are few comic scenes in his theatre, although they do exist. In *Man, the Beast and Virtue* (1906), there is a sequence which will, if well performed, arouse laughter in the stalls. Paolino has had an affair with a virtuous if gormless young woman while her ferocious husband is at sea. She has fallen pregnant, and to avoid disaster for them both, Paolino teaches her the arts of seduction to help her entice her husband to make love to her on his return, allowing the baby to be plausibly passed off as his. The somewhat feckless woman has the unfortunate and unbeguiling habit of letting her mouth hang open, so Paolino has to give her instructions on how to smile and maximise her allure. The comedy may be viewed as heartless and cold, but such passages are rare, and are in any case not what Pirandello means by 'humour'.

Humour and comedy have to be rigorously distinguished, as Pirandello illustrates with a remarkable, delicate parable which would have graced any of his short stories:

> I see an elderly woman, with her hair dyed and greased over by some kind of revolting concoction, and she herself clumsily glamorised and done up in clothes too young for her. I start laughing. *I am aware* that that elderly lady is the *contrary* of what a respectable old lady ought to be. I can, at first sight and superficially, stop at that comic impression. The comic is precisely the *awareness of contradiction*. But if reflection were now to intervene and suggest to me that that elderly woman perhaps feels no enjoyment in doing herself up like a parrot, but that she might be suffering on account of it and does so only because, pitiably, she deludes herself that, done up in that style, concealing her wrinkles and grey hair, she will succeed in retaining the love of a husband who is much younger than her, then at that point I can no longer laugh as before, precisely because reflection, working inside me, has made me go beyond, or rather more deeply inside, that first awareness: from the initial *awareness of contradiction* it has made me move to a *feeling of contradiction*. And it is here that the difference between the comic

and the humorous lies. (p. 126; author's emphases)

This fundamental passage is worth detailed analysis. The reasoning is based on a series of distinctions or dualities:

| | |
|---|---|
| comedy | humour |
| spontaneous | reflective |
| *awareness of contradiction* | *feeling of contradiction* |
| laughter | pity |

Comedy is a trivial, frivolous, perhaps even sadistic reaction to a spectacle which presents itself as incongruous, or 'contradictory'. In that sense, *Man, the Beast and Virtue* can be categorised as comedy, not humour. The place of laughter in this discussion is equivocal. Laughter is a property of the human animal alone but there are different kinds and grades of laughter. The contemporary playwright Dario Fo pointed out that in antiquity the moment when a baby first laughs was regarded as the moment it acquired some awareness of its own humanity. 'A baby's first smile is viewed as the birth of intelligence, or even as the moment of infusion of the soul. Laughter is sacred,' he said.[1] Not all laughter is so innocent. The laughter occasioned by sparkling wit is not the laughter of seeing a bully or hypocrite hoist with his own petard. Other classifications would include the cordial outburst of sheer happiness when friends meet, the contented chuckle, the guffaw in response to a joke, but also the derisive laughter of scorn which is the expression of power over a fellow creature who is thus denied respect. In addition, there can be an element of cruelty, even sadism, in seemingly innocuous laughter. The most common gag in silent cinema was the 'banana skin' joke, when some innocent was sent hurtling to the floor by a slippery skin. In day-to-day life, such a person would merit sympathy and help, but at a safe distance, in a fixed context, and provided the accident occurs to someone else, such a situation can appear funny, although scarcely

[1] Joseph Farrell, *Dario Fo and Franca Rame: Harlequins of the Revolution* (London, Methuen, 2001), p. 277.

harmless. Pirandello retains the term 'comedy' for that initial, unmediated and superficial response which is close to jeering. In the unkind language used in English, the woman behaving as does the woman in Pirandello's fable could be described as 'mutton dressed as lamb'. She was the object of heartless, hurtful laughter.

The factor which allows an observer to transcend that superficial stage is thought or reflection. The observer stops to consider that there may be a motive, perhaps some private unhappiness, behind this strange, incongruous public conduct. The dress and odd appearance of the woman in question may be the expression of something more than conceit, and in those circumstances it may transpire that the object of laughter deserves not derision but compassion. The observer then passes from mere *awareness* to the dimension of *feeling*, although emotion or sentiment would be equally good translations. Pirandello explains his meaning with an extract from Dostoevsky's *Crime and Punishment* where Marmeladov, addressing Raskolnikov in a hostelry in Moscow, tells him: 'Perhaps you, like the others, find all this *ridiculous*: perhaps I am boring you telling you all these miserable and stupid details of my domestic life, but for me it is not *ridiculous*. I *feel* all this . . .'. Feeling is here fellow feeling, identification with another's suffering, sympathy or compassion in the most literal, etymological sense of the word. It is a recognition of a common humanity. Humour and pity go hand in hand. Writing in the same essay on Don Abbondio, a weak, cowardly priest and a somewhat ridiculous figure in Alessandro Manzoni's historical novel, *The Betrothed*, Pirandello states that Manzoni does not dismiss his character with contempt, however pusillanimous he may be. 'Yes, Manzoni has pity for this poor man who is Don Abbondio; but it is a pity which at the same time wreaks havoc, of necessity. In fact, only by laughing at him and making people laugh at him can he pity him and make him pitied, show compassion and make him the object of compassion' (p. 145).

If pity is the moral virtue which is a component of

humorous art, it does not exhaust the meaning of the term. The humorous vision is of its essence a realisation of a world awry and of times which are out of joint, where the only credible response is an amused, puzzled, wry state of mind. This humour is a product of disorientation, of an 'inability to know where to turn, a perplexity, an irresolution of the conscience' (p. 147). The humorous observer lacks the facile certainties of the comic onlooker. This disenchanted, disorientated turn of mind is displayed by Leone Gala in *The Rules of the Game*, the play the actors in *Six Characters in Search of an Author* are rehearsing when the characters arrive. Gala has been abandoned by his wife but to maintain appearances goes every day to the house where she resides with her lover. He expresses his view of his own condition in a series of sardonic witticisms. Lucidly aware that his behaviour and the life he is forced to live are eccentric and bizarre, he widens his personal sense of his grotesque condition to make it a generalised view of all life on earth. He treats his uncomprehending servant, ironically nicknamed Socrates, to discourses on the philosophy of Henri Bergson and its inadequacy for explaining the relations between reason and reality, but he himself views all life and all philosophies of life as charades. Not all Pirandello's humorous characters have Gala's level of insight and self-awareness. In *The Turn* (1902), Pirandello's second novel, a man decides to give his daughter in marriage not to the young man she loves but to an elderly villager who had been married three times previously. The decisive fact is that the father's motivation is love of his daughter. He believes that the new husband will soon die, leaving her his wealth and allowing the man she really loves to have his 'turn' as her husband. The disbelief and derision of the villagers when his schemes are made public will not bend him from his plan. The results are different from the intentions, and his single-minded stubbornness creates havoc and victims.

The society portrayed is not governed by rationality or common sense, and can be depicted only in the disbelieving, distancing and incredulous terms in which the great humorist writers, such as W. M. Thackeray (whom Pirandello mentions, p. 29), Mark Twain (whom he admired)[1] or Nikolai Gogol, have portrayed it. All tend to view the 'Vanity Fair' of life with a jaundiced eye, to contemplate the doings of their fellow men and women wryly and perhaps ironically, to shake their heads at the spectacle presented to them. It might be helpful to recall a statement by Gogol: 'I am destined by the mysterious powers to walk hand in hand with my strange heroes, viewing life in all its immensity as it rushes by me, viewing it through laughter seen by the world and tears unseen and unknown by it.'[2] These words are very much in keeping with Pirandello's own:

> The most common, and yet most generally observed, characteristics are the fundamental 'contradiction', whose principal cause is normally given as the discord which meditation and sentiment uncover either between real life and the ideal or between our aspirations and weaknesses and miseries, and whose principal effect is that perplexity between tears and laughter. (p. 121)

That mixture of tears and bitter laughter is strongly present in Pirandello, whose vision is more pessimistic than that of the others mentioned. The world, being barren and purposeless, provides no grounds for optimism, hope or belief in the prospect of joy. The first impulse might be laughter at the senselessness of it all, but this reaction has to be quickly stifled as inappropriate. Seeing life as bizarre or absurd (the term 'absurd' became common in the later phase of European history and philosophy, with French post-Second World War existentialism), and savouring the realisation of the incongruity of existence are the bases of Pirandellian humour. The notion of 'incongruity' is the key:

[1] Interview with Domenico Vittorini (Vittorini, 1958, p. 165).
[2] Nikolai Gogol, *Dead Souls*, trans. David Magarshack (Harmondsworth, Penguin, 1961), p. 143.

Pirandello's word is *contrario*, a cosmic contradiction or contrariness which is intrinsic to human experience. The humorist's vision provides the only bearable response to life as Pirandello conceives it, as he says it must be conceived. Pirandello's subject, in his fiction and his theatre, is something as grand and overarching as the mystery of life itself. He is one of those titanic writers who had the expansive ambition to take the life, death and quest for meaning of the rational human being on earth as his subject, but he does not approach it with reverence.

His view of the panorama facing that human being during the short period of consciousness granted them, or on the short journey in time, was stark. He entitled a couple of brief autobiographical pages 'The involuntary Sojourn on Earth of Luigi Pirandello'. There was no hope or consolation to be had from religion, or from any human achievement. Human beings have, as he makes clear in 'On Humour', the advantage and disadvantage of being endowed with reason, since this faculty makes them, uniquely among mortal creatures, aware of their predicament and mortality. Life has no meaning or purpose in itself, but human beings must struggle to attach to it their own values and objectives, though these will be illusory. It does not matter what that purpose is, since 'it cannot be the true purpose [. . .] what matters is that importance is given to something, however vain that may be: it will be worth as much as another purpose considered more serious, because in the last analysis neither one nor the other will give satisfaction' (pp. 138–9). The purpose of the publicity-seeker, in other words, trying to see how many people he can jam into a medium-sized telephone box is as good as that of a saint endeavouring to feed the hungry. There is no given hierarchy of values.

That realisation of the nullity of things makes Pirandellian humour necessary. The humorous spirit can derive from personal sadness, from the 'special disposition of human reflection', from 'an innate or inherited melancholy' or from a 'bitter experience of life, or a pessimism, or a scepticism acquired by study or by consideration of the lot of human existence' (p. 133). The old certainties of religion, ethics, philosophy and politics have crumbled, leaving men and women to face an empty universe in which there is no stability, and above all in which life has no coherence and 'fatally for human reason, no clear and determined purpose' (p. 138). Humour is an alternative to despair for humanity, since humanity is, as he wrote in 'Art and Conscience Today', published in the same year as 'On Humour', suspended 'in mystery and without God' (p. 890). The characteristics of modern life as Pirandello saw it are:

> egoism, moral lassitude, lack of courage in the face of adversities, pessimism, nausea, self-disgust, indolence, incapacity of the will, levity, extraordinary emotional abandon, suggestibility, unconscious mendacity, facile excitability, a mania for imitation and a boundless overestimation of their own worth. (*Saggi e scritti vari*, p. 875)

The 'boundless overestimation of their own worth' is a provocation to a humorist, for whom an overinflated sense of self-importance is an invitation to a debunking prank which will deflate metaphysical as well as social pretension. Humour is predicated on the recognition of a world 'off key', in his own phrase, *Off Key* being also the title of a volume of poetry which appeared in 1912. Harmony has been shattered, the comfortable connections between hopes and vision have been fractured. Pity for the beings caught up in this shipwreck alone survives. Humour is as much a moral as an aesthetic category, springing from a will to display to human beings the smallness and insignificance of their aspirations, appetites or needs in a world which takes little account of them. It is in this spirit that Pirandello identifies as one of the great humorists, even if unintentionally, Copernicus, the Danish scientist who first asserted that the earth was a minor planet which rotated round the sun and thus not the centre of the universe. In a

Copernican universe, humanity is not a privileged being at the peak of a hierarchy of creation, residing in the very heart of the cosmos, but an insignificant creature placed on a mobile celestial body hurtling round a sun. The achievement of Copernicus was not so much that he had 'dismantled the machine of the universe as the conceited image that we had made of it'.

> The discovery of the telescope gave us the final blow: another infernal device that can be paired with the one given to us by nature. But this one we invented ourselves. While the eye looks from below, from the smaller lens, and sees as great that which nature had providentially meant us to see as small, what does our soul do? It leaps up to look from above, from the bigger lens, and the telescope then becomes a dreadful instrument, which brings down earth, and man and all our glories and grandeurs.
>
> As luck would have it, it is one of the properties of humorous reflection to provoke the sense of contradiction, which in the present case says – But is man really as little as the wrong end of the telescope makes us see him? [. . .] But it is equally true that if he then feels himself to be great and a humorist gets to know about it, he could end up like Gulliver, a giant in Lilliput and a plaything in the hands of the giants in Brodingnag. (pp. 159–60)

The six characters are playthings in the hands of their God, the author who creates them then cuts them adrift, yet the Father insists that they are Gullivers compared to the human beings. The Father, with his awareness of the fragility of the life of human beings, is the figure who most strongly embodies the humorist vision, and it is he too who appeals most strongly for pity and understanding of his own predicament, even if the others, the victims of his conduct, have a stronger claim to it. Cruelty and the plea for compassion are continually offset one against the other. The laughter of the actors is answered by the tears of the characters.

## Characters and characterisation

Finding the appropriate vocabulary for discussing the cast of 'characters' who appear in *Six Characters in Search of an Author* presents difficulties which will not be encountered with virtually any other play, since in a Pirandellian world view the category 'character' is contrasted with the category 'actor', or indeed 'human being' in general. The play debates the clash between illusion and reality, and even proposes the radical thesis that illusion *is* reality. The deep meaning of the play is expressed in the paradox that the actors and human beings cannot reach the same level of reality as the invented characters. Plainly, inside a real theatre for an actual production of the work, the dilemmas of the 'characters' have to be brought to life by actors, but to some extent that validates Pirandello's premise: human beings act and don masks in day-to-day life, while characters simply and unselfconsciously exist.

Similarly there are problems in talking of a 'play', since the reference may be to the published and performed work as it left Pirandello's desk, or to the theatre-within-theatre, the unwritten and unrealised drama which the characters yearn to live. For clarity, we shall refer to an outer play, being the encounter in the theatre between the six characters and the theatre people, and an inner play, meaning the drama which these characters carry within them. There are also two sharply contrasted dimensions of being – the characters and the actors, including in this latter category the Producer. Madame Pace, while having much in common with the characters, exists in a realm of her own, and the Father, the Stepdaughter and the Producer have the nous and insight to open dialogue across the gulf.

### *The characters*

There are certain factors, fundamental to their being, which unite the six characters, while the nature of the drama they yearn to perform, which involves acts of treachery, desertion, abuse and deceit, giving rise to bitter reproaches and recrimination, will tear them apart. The characters' differing demands, their shared quest for life and their individual need for the expression of their private emotional and intellectual being impose on the play a swing-pendulum development, where moments of solidarity are followed by scenes of lacerating division. The names they are given indicate only, but crucially, relationships inside a family, the site of most Pirandello's dramas. The family can be described as 'bourgeois', 'patriarchal' or 'dysfunctional', since all three adjectives apply.

If Pirandello failed to find in the characters' story the 'universal value' he required of a work of theatre, he did nonetheless, as he writes in the Preface, locate that value in their quest for an author and hence for life, and in their ability as a group to 'express as their own living passion' the questions which had tormented him, questions on Life and Form, on multiple personality and on communication. Pirandello had not, obviously, spurned the characters themselves, but he had eschewed 'their drama, which undoubtedly interested them above all else, but did not at all interest me' (Preface, p. 210). They are all in the desperate and impossible situation of craving to represent their drama, the only one of which they are capable, but which the author, the source of their being, has rejected as inadequate for a man of his outlook. 'They are all six at the same point of artistic realisation and on the same level of reality, which is the fantastic level of the whole play. Except that the Father, the Stepdaughter and also the Son are realised as mind; the Mother as nature; the Boy as a presence watching and performing a gesture and the Little Girl unaware of it all.' In seeming contradiction, he then adds, 'I had the impression that some of them needed to be fully realised (artistically speaking) and others less so, and others merely sketched in as elements of a narrative or presentational sequence' (ibid., p. 208). Critics are united that the level of imaginative force in the presentation of the characters is not uniform and that the Father and

Stepdaughter have a level of imagined life denied the others.

*The Father*

He is in many ways the central character both of the encounter with the actors which constitutes the framing play and of the tragedy of the characters which is the inner play. Often described as taking the role of *raisonneur*, that is, the character who can be regarded as the author's spokesperson, or who describes from his own point of view the development and sense of the drama. He has a tendency to lecture, and acts as messenger between the two worlds of characters and actors. His awareness of his ill-defined status as unwritten character causes him enormous pain, and it is he who, together with the Stepdaughter, leads the search for an author. This plight as character-without-author he endures as an 'inexplicable tragedy and as a situation he tries with all his powers to rebel against' (ibid., p. 211). Endowed with a subtly elaborated view of the human condition and a high measure of articulacy, it is he who engages the Producer in dialogue to try and entice him to act as substitute for the renegade author. He is the main exponent of Pirandellism, expatiating on the limits of theatre, the nature of a character and the mysteries of creativity, the paradoxical superiority of the character over the human, on the conflicts between the mask and face and between life and form.

However, this sense of the tragedy of the mask is an exquisite example of Pirandellian intellectual suffering converted into passion. The Father proclaims his aspiration to high moral standards, but the mask imposed on him by his Stepdaughter, and accepted by the others, is of a priapic lecher. The Pirandellian dilemma of the clash between mask and face becomes the human complaint of a man given an image by one specific, shameful action which is, he pleads, out of character. The stage directions at the entrance of the characters indicate that his dominant personality trait is remorse, and his overwhelming drive is for self-explanation and self-justification, but the Stepdaughter, the victim of his sexual desires, is determined to ensure that a mask of shame remains in place. He wishes to present himself as altruistic in his conduct towards his wife and motivated by the Daemon of Experiment, but the Stepdaughter views him as pusillanimous and self-serving, prone to perceive 'the beast in man, but then excuse it'. He is aware of his own depravity and is no liar, but he is trapped, and may very well be guilty of self-delusion over his own motives.

Any attempt to construct a psychological profile and social background for him would have to take cognisance of the fact that he was plainly a prosperous member of the upper bourgeoisie – he was able to employ a secretary and had a big house – and that he was an intellectual with a firm grounding in philosophic conjecture. He is the main cause of the tragedies which have befallen the family. It was he who forced together the Mother and the secretary, he who sent the Son away from home, he whose voyeurism on the Stepdaughter caused the new family to move town, he whose desires led to the fateful meeting in Madame Pace's, he whose inability to explain the new situation to the Son led to the tensions in the home when the Mother and her children came back to live with him, he who cannot find any outlet for his guilt. All this in addition to his dominant role in the negotiations with the Producer.

*The Mother*

Pirandello is insistent that this woman is to be seen as a mother and not as a wife, lover or even woman. Her femininity is denied: 'she's not a woman, she's a mother', the Father explains to the presumably bemused Producer. The effect is that she is not permitted any savour of sexual feeling, or even of the emotion of non-maternal love. When the Father discusses the moves which led to her leaving the marital home and moving in with the secretary, with whom she shares feelings of tenderness, he is very insistent that this is not a re-run of romantic tales of the eternal triangle. Her story must not be seen as a sentimental drama of a woman emotionally torn between conjugal obligations and illicit, adulterous love. There was no shortage of such stories in Victorian literature, even by the greatest of writers, such as Tolstoy (*Anna Karenina*) and Flaubert (*Madame Bovary*). This is not her plight. She is essentially passive, asexual, cowed, resigned to her role in life and not given to challenges and questions.

In his Preface, Pirandello defines her as being realised as 'nature', unlike the Father who is realised as 'mind'. 'She is never aware of being a character inasmuch as she is never, even for a moment, detached from her role. She does not know she has a role.' She is an elemental force, with little intelligence. She advances no explanation of what has befallen her, and has no particular insight to propose. She can't compete with her husband, and rarely intervenes to offer corrections. 'Her role as mother does not of itself, in its natural essence, embrace mental activity. And she does not exist as a mind' (pp. 211–12). Her husband says that he had been drawn to her precisely because of her 'humility', which in Italian may indicate either her poor background or some trait of her personality. In his description of her in the introductory stage directions, Pirandello emphasises that the fundamental emotion her mask portrays is 'sorrow'. If she were wearing an actual, physical mask it would have 'wax tears' which could recall, in Pirandello's own words, the *mater dolorosa* of Catholic iconography. She is, in other words, like the Virgin Mary at the Passion and Crucifixion of her son, Jesus. The Mother's suffering stems largely from the attitude her Son adopts towards her, since that undermines her position as mother. She is a picture of suffering motherhood, with few individual distinguishing traits.

While it is easy to see this character in Pirandellian terms, there is something enigmatic and troubling about this depiction. She is a figure hauntingly representative of an ancient Mediterranean culture, where women had a fixed place in society, and were the object of sexual desire but were not permitted to be desiring subjects. The 'mother' occupied an identifiable place in the hierarchy of Mediterranean, including Sicilian, life, a place which had privilege and power combined with restrictions. The mother was the 'angel of the hearth', but not expected to display needs of her own. Her principal task was the care of, and relationship with, her children, especially sons. This relationship has broken down for the Mother, and it is this, not the heartlessness of the Father, which is the cause of her suffering. Never is Pirandello both more Pirandellian and more Sicilian than in the depiction of this character.

*The Stepdaughter*

It has often been said that women in Italian literature are of two kinds – the Madonna and the whore. Whatever the general truth of the proposition, the Mother and the Stepdaughter have the misfortune to illustrate this dichotomy.

Not that the Stepdaughter chose to be a prostitute. Her position 'on the pavement' and in Madame Pace's service was brought about by circumstances not of her making, and in a spirit of desperate self-sacrifice she accepted this work to provide for her mother and her brother and sister. As seen in the drama, she is out to make herself mistress of her own fate and to exact revenge on those, primarily the Father but also the Son, who are responsible for her predicament. Curiously, although she shares a dominant role with the Father both inside the family and towards the Producer, Pirandello has little to say about her in his Preface. He agrees that she, like the Father, should be regarded as 'mind', and it is clear from the progress of the play that her need to find expression is as urgent as the Father's. The nature of the mask suggested for her in the stage directions make clear why: she wants revenge on the Father for the humiliation of that encounter in Madame Pace's shop and for all the hardship he had caused the family. She is determined to deny him any facile self-exculpation, and is especially relentless in her pursuit of him when he spins some complex philosophical yarn about how misunderstood he is and how inappropriate is the mask she imposes on him for a man of his moral sense. Her feelings towards the rest of the family are not of uniform tenderness. She is protective towards the two little children, but contemptuous of the Son and irritated at the Mother's inability to control her feelings for this young man who has disowned her.

*The Son*

The Son is marked by a sense of haughty superiority deriving from his legitimacy and consequent sense of not belonging to the rabble that his family has become. For this reason he is reluctant to be tarred with the same brush and makes every effort to remain on the sidelines in both the outer and inner play. He takes little part in the efforts of the Father and Stepdaughter to have the drama enacted, and even initially attempts, futilely, to escape when one of the scenes involving the characters is about to be staged. Escape is impossible, since his part (his life) is preordained by virtue of his status as a character in the one (unwritten) story. This does not give him any fondness for that role, or any tolerance of the family's drama. Pirandello writes that the essence of this character is that he 'denies the drama which makes him a character', that is, the play involving the characters, and indeed that he 'draws his importance and value from being a character *not* in that play' (p. 216). Pirandello continues, 'In short, he is the only one who lives solely as a "character in search of an author" – inasmuch as the author he seeks is not a dramatic author.' He exists in the framework of the search, trying to evade his part in the characters' own play and even making every effort to frustrate the quest to involve the Producer. He announces towards the climax of the play that the author was right to suppress the story of that family. However, he contributes significantly to the evolving tragedy of the characters themselves. His attitude towards the Stepdaughter determines the nature of family relations once they are all back in the Father's house, and it is his decision to withdraw sullenly to his room, compelling the Mother to come seeking him, which leaves the little children unprotected, causing the Girl to drown and the Boy to shoot himself.

If, in terms of Pirandellism, he has the one mask expressing scorn, and is unable to escape either from the drama or from his responsibilities, it is also legitimate to see him in less abstract terms. Psychologically, he is a young man who has been damaged by parental, especially paternal, neglect and denial of affection. He had been sent away from the home at an impressionable age for reasons which remain obscure. The Father, whose good faith can be doubted, claims to have been acting in the boy's best interests and to have striven to ensure that he grew up in touch with nature, but the Stepdaughter, who is scarcely any more of an objective witness, asserts that the Father simply wanted to rid himself of responsibilities. There is no need to be a Freudian psychotherapist to appreciate that such rejection at a young age is likely to have calamitous consequences on the unformed psyche, and will lead to the emotional aridity which the Son displays. There is no way of knowing when he returned to his Father's home, but safely installed there in adolescence, he was witness to what he believed to be a sexual relationship between his father and an unknown young woman whom he discovers only later to be his half-sister, but a half-sister who had made contact with the Father in compromising and shaming circumstances. His withdrawal from the family and his refusal of close relations with them can be seen in psychological terms which owe nothing to Pirandellism.

*The Boy and Girl*

Neither has a speaking part, and little can be known about them as individuals. In the Preface, Pirandello tells us that the Boy is 'a presence' and the Girl is 'unaware' of it all. He adds that 'the two children have hardly any substance beyond their appearance, and need to be led by the hand' (p. 209). However, the stage directions make the Boy surprisingly old; fourteen is Pirandello's suggested age, although most modern directors tend to have him played as younger. What kind of 'presence' do they represent? They cannot articulate any dilemma or even any pain and protest of their own, but are the haunting conscience, the wholly innocent victims of the tragedy. Born of the union of the Mother and the secretary, they are viewed with scorn by the Son, with indifference by the Father, and while the Girl receives the affection of the Stepdaughter, the Boy does not. Even the Mother favours the Son over them. They have disappeared when the re-formed family of Father, Mother and Son exit from the theatre at the end. They do not even make their escape with the Stepdaughter, their full sister.

They are the silent, reproachful presences of the play, orphaned by the death of their father, uncomprehending of the events around them, plainly hurt and harmed by the treatment they had received and stunted in their emotional growth. The Boy appears to have watched unconcerned while his sister drowned herself, making him some kind of accessory to her death. He then shoots himself, having previously armed himself with a gun. The crushing of innocence is a spectacle and a metaphor used by several writers in the realist tradition, and they are victims of the inner, 'realist' play Pirandello declines to write, but have no part in the outer play involving the meeting in the theatre.

*Madame Pace*

It may be that some image involving her represented the first conception of the whole story in Pirandello's imagination. The only remaining extract of the novel which was the first form of the story deals with the scene in her shop, but while she is exercising the same professions, dressmaker and procuress, as in the play, she is a more conventional Signora Pace and seems to have no Spanish connections.

In spite of her brief appearance, Madame Pace is the most enigmatic character in the piece and her contribution is of immense importance. She is not one of the six characters, even if she is associated with them, and is certainly not one of the actors. She exists in a dimension of her own, appearing almost magically in a way which defies laws of nature and verisimilitude but which does obey rules of a theatre divorced from any obligation to offer a facsimile of life. She remains a phantasm, a creature of a fantasy world and as such is a challenge to any realist aesthetic. She is the only character to be given a name in the cast list. *Pace* is the Italian for peace, but she hardly emerges as a pacifier. She is made gracelessly comic by the idiom, a pigeon version of Spanish-Italian, she uses. Perhaps she can be viewed, as Eric Bentley suggests, as the antithesis of the Mother, the equivalent of the wicked stepmother of fairy tales. 'She is motherhood degraded and she is sex degraded' (Bentley, 1972, p. 53).

*The Producer*

In modern theatre jargon, this man would be the director, the organising spirit and interpreter behind the entire production. However, this figure had been unknown to Italian theatre until Pirandello's lifetime and Pirandello tended to treat him with some suspicion. Such was the novelty of the role filled by the director that there was no accepted term for him. The Italian word used by Pirandello in the cast list for this play was *direttore-capocomico*, where *capocomico* was the traditional term employed in *commedia dell'arte*, and meant literally 'lead actor'. The term which gained acceptance is *regista*, the title Pirandello confers on the theatre-in-theatre director in the later *Tonight We Improvise* (1930). The *capocomico* was the dominant figure in the *commedia dell'arte* tradition, and fulfilled many of the tasks now assigned to the director – choice of script, distribution of parts, design of sets, arrangement of scenes – but he was also the principal performer in the company. The director in the modern sense appeared first in Germany, and arrived in Italy later than in other European countries. The Producer in this play is this more modern figure who oversees rehearsal and the production process without taking on an acting role.

The characters recognise the dominant role of the Producer when they make him, not the cast, their first point of contact. They suggest that he could extend his influence by acting as a surrogate author. The Producer is bemused by the suggestion, but he displays throughout a keen sense of theatre and stagecraft. He insists on respect for the integrity of the author's script.[1] He may be limited in his outlook, but to caricature him as a blinkered, bourgeois fool is to miss the point. He does not have the subtlety or insight of the Father, but he does ensure that the Father has to be on his mettle. The actors treat him with respect, and his account of the nature and appeal of theatre and acting is deeply felt and well turned. His interpretation of Pirandello's *The Rules of the Game* is accurate, even if he makes a joke of it. On the other hand, he is no revolutionary. He has no ambition to question the conventions of his own time, and has no hesitation in, for example, telling the Stepdaughter that on stage 'truth's all

[1] Roberto Alonge, *Luigi Pirandello* (Bari, Laterza, 1997), p. 50.

very well up to a point, but . . .'. Equally, he will not allow his actors to adopt stereotypes, and encourages the leading actor to show more 'subtlety' in his depiction of the Father and not reduce him to some well-meaning, elderly gent. Alone among the theatre professionals, he has the ability to hold a dialogue with the characters and grasp something of their predicament and attempt to convert it into theatre. However, he lacks the flexibility and originality to rise fully to the challenge and work out the new techniques and philosophy which would be needed for this unprecedented situation.

*The actors*

The rest of the theatre professionals can be lumped together. None of them emerges in their own right, and none displays any of the sensitivity which would be needed to do justice to a depiction of the characters' dilemma. At this point in his development, Pirandello did not have a high regard for actors. In his earlier 'Illustrators, Actors and Translators' (1908), he wrote off actors as a necessary but regrettable obstacle to communication between writer and audience, and in his correspondence with Virginio Talli, the great actor-manager who staged some of Pirandello's early plays, he lamented the lack of brio, the vanity and self-interest of actors as a whole.[1] That would appear to be the case with all the actors in this play. The leading lady is conceited and vacuous, the leading man needs detailed instructions on how to approach the character, and none of them gives evidence of insight or intelligence. Pirandello depicts them in such a way that none of them contributes to advancing the play-within-the-play or making its outlines clearer. Their flatness is in marked contrast to the vivacity of the Father and the Stepdaughter.

[1] Quoted in *Maschere Nude*, ed. Alessandro D'Amico (Milan, Mondadori, 1986 and 1993), vol. 2, p. 222.

## Writing and performance history

It has often been the complaint of writers that they are not accorded the privilege given to painters or composers of returning to a motif or embellishing a theme once touched on. There is no shortage of examples in the history of art of artists reworking subjects even after decades, from Michelangelo's four versions of the Pietà to Picasso's many paintings of the figure of Pierrot. In literature, on the other hand, a writer is criticised if he repeats himself, if he fails to start afresh with every work or to leave his past behind and move on.

Pirandello did not respect this rule, choosing to rework, expand and deepen in theatre situations plots which had their origin in short stories he had previously written and published. The short story should, in the view of Guy de Maupassant, one of the masters of the genre, be sufficiently crisp and concise as to be able to be read at one sitting, and be sufficiently focused to allow the reader to rise from the chair with that one emotion or thought in his mind. Drama, on the other hand, provides an arena for a deeper clash and more subtle interplay between opposing forces or between characters with contrasting viewpoints, so that the transposition from page to stage can never be merely a question of simply transferring and extending dialogue, or of writing in one or two additional parts. The core idea in a short story of his was, frequently, adapted by Pirandello in a play written perhaps a decade later. The play staged under the title *If Not So* in 1915, and given its definitive title *Other People's Reasons* in 1921, was based on an idea developed in a short story published as 'The Kite' as far back as 1896. The 1920 play *As Before, Better Than Before* was inspired by a story entitled 'The Vigil', published in 1904. *The Wives' Friend* went on stage in 1927 but the short story of the same name had first appeared in 1894. The modifications the basic notions had undergone in the intervening years are intriguing, but so too is the significant continuity of outlook in Pirandello.

Both continuity and change are apparent in the

successive structures which encase the dilemmas and ideas debated in *Six Characters in Search of an Author*. Among authors, Pirandello plainly belonged, like Tolstoy, to those endowed with a keen sense of the physicality and concrete being of his characters. He saw them vividly and keenly, and provided in his writing detailed accounts of, for example, their style of walking, their habits of eating and their odd ways of closing their eyes when listening to people speaking. His created characters were not shadowy creatures, mental ciphers or vague projections of some problem he wished to discuss. There are accounts given by people who frequented Pirandello's house of seeing him in animated debate in a room which was seemingly empty but which in his eyes was filled with the characters who would people his fiction. He was overheard urging these imaginary beings to consider other points of view and even pausing to listen to their replies.

Other writers have toyed with the idea of depicting their characters in the moments of liberty when they are released from the roles created for them. R. L. Stevenson, for instance, has a short story in which while he himself stops for lunch, Long John Silver and Benn Gunn from *Treasure Island* settle down for a pipe and a chat, only to scarper back inside their familiar roles when the writer sits down at his desk. With Stevenson, this was an escapade of whimsy, divorced from his serious work as a novelist. With Pirandello, such considerations on the level of being accorded characters, and the extent to which that being reflected or contrasted with life as humans lived it, were central to his thinking. It could be said that the fundamental ideas and dilemmas which underlie *Six Characters* were in search of a form for a period of between fifteen and twenty years. The notion appeared in several short stories, the first entitled simply 'Characters', published in a periodical in 1906 but never subsequently republished in any of his collections. The opening lines read:

> Today, a hearing.
>
> I receive from 9 to 12, in my study, the ladies and gentlemen

> who will be characters in my future stories.
> Such types!
> I really do not know why all the malcontents of life have to present themselves to me. If I treated them well, I would understand. But I treat them like dogs. And they know that I am not easy to please, that I am cruelly curious, that I will not allow myself to be fooled by appearances or tricked by chatter [. . .] But they all have, or believe they have (which is the same), a particular unhappiness to set out and they come to me, petulantly, to beg for voice and life.[1]

The individual characters are introduced into his room by a servant called Fantasy, who will appear under the same name and exercising the same profession in the Preface to *Six Characters*. While no one in the tale has any resemblance to the later six characters in the play, their principal spokesman, a physicist by the name of Leandro Scoto, expresses an outlook which prefigures that of the Father. He begs for that level of life granted him by the circumstances of his birth, but has to listen to the author tell them: 'Art, ladies and gentlemen, has the duty of rendering souls immobile, of fixing life in one moment or in various determined moments: the statue in a gesture, the countryside in a temporary, immutable appearance. But what a torture!' Scoto puts the author in the story on the spot with the first formulation of that paradox which will recur in Pirandello. Whereas some fictional characters may be merely ephemeral, he says, others are immortal, but all have the inestimable, undeniable privilege of 'true life, more true than real life'. The higher truth they incarnate derives from the fact that they, unlike creatures who have their being in 'real life', are immune to all change. Characters exist in a dimension outside history and are free of the wasting effects of time; they are not subject to the accidents or incidentals of life. They live by the very essence of their nature.

[1] Appendix to *Sei personaggi in cerca d'autore*, ed. Guido Davico Bonino (Turin, Einaudi, 1993), p. 161.

The characters who crowd his room demanding audience in a later short story, 'The Tragedy of a Character' (1911), similarly complain of the author's cruelty in refusing them life, while the author wonders why they should aspire to the kind of life a man of his persuasion would be likely to give them. By now the ideas set out in 'On Humour' had become an integral part of Pirandello's philosophy of life, so it is no surprise to hear the author in the story tell the aspiring characters, who are still prey to discontent and unhappiness, that since he is 'fundamentally good-hearted' he will accord them pity, but then explain the very Pirandellian dilemma over how to depict their misery. 'How is compassion for certain misfortunes possible except by laughing at them?' The main fictional character demanding a hearing is one Dr Fileno, a thinker who had written a work entitled *The Philosophy of the Distant*, in which he advocates seeing problems of the present as though through the wrong end of a telescope, but he has also a deep awareness of his predicament as a character. He tells the author:

> No one knows better than you that we are living beings, more alive than those who breathe and wear clothes: perhaps less real but more true. One can be born to life in so many ways, my dear sir; and you are well aware that nature makes use of the instrument of human fantasy to continue her work of creation. And anyone who is born to life thanks to this creative activity which resides in the spirit of man is ordained by nature to a life far superior to that of a person who emerges from the mortal womb of a woman. Anyone born of fantasy can snap his fingers even at death.[1]

The third story, 'Conversations with Characters' (1915), makes use of the same setting, although on this occasion the author puts on his study door a notice banning, on account of the grimness of the times, all further conversation with characters. The tale is more openly

[1] Ibid., p. 170.

autobiographical. The fictional author, like Pirandello himself, is depressed over the outbreak of the European war and over the prospect of his son being called to fight on the Austrian front. The insistent character who manages to force his way into his room tries to divert the writer by calling attention to the song of the birds and the flowering of the plants in the garden, and suggests that art should concern itself with 'matters which are higher than the transitory passions of today'. The plea is of no avail, since on this occasion the author believes that the debts to be paid to history are more urgent. In other tales, for instance 'The Bat', actors in rehearsal are compelled to face the conflict between the fiction to which they are giving life and the reality which imposes itself on them, but not, as might be the case with other writers, in order to confront the frivolity of the fictional world they temporarily inhabit but so as to ponder their own fragility and tenuous grasp on life, as compared to that given to Sancho Panza, Hamlet, Orestes by literature.

Pirandello's own need to confront this question in a more extended form could not be resisted, but his first plan was to incorporate the story of the six characters in a novel. In July 1917, he wrote to his son Stefano, still a prisoner-of-war in Austria:

> My head is already so full of new things! So many stories [. . .] and one strange business which is so sad, so sad: *Six Characters in Search of an Author*: a novel in the making. Perhaps you understand. Six characters, caught up in a terrible drama, who present themselves to me to be included in a novel, an obsession, and I want nothing to do with them, and I tell them it's useless and I don't care about them and I don't care about anything, and they show me their wounds and I throw them out [. . .] and so finally the novel in the making will be done.[1]

There is no way of knowing why and when Pirandello decided a play was a more appropriate vehicle for this

[1] Ibid., p. 183.

'strange business' than a novel, but the script in its first form was completed by early 1921. Pirandello's name is more closely linked to this work than to any other production of his, and he was aware from the outset that he had produced a work of startling, indeed revolutionary originality. He invited directors, actors and critics to hear him reading his newly completed script, with himself taking all the parts. Dario Niccodemi, who would be director of the first production, has left an account of hearing Pirandello reading the script in his house in Rome, and has recorded his astonishment at the 'vehemence in the reading. What a whirlwind; what an overwhelming tumult of words, sounds, yells. There is no resisting him [. . .] with his fists banging energetically on the page as though to underline certain words and make them lodge in the mind of the listeners, as though he were hammering a nail into hard wood, Luigi Pirandello seems to read more for himself than for others.'[1] Significantly, he added 'admiration began where understanding left off', and confessed that at the end 'we were bewildered, in chaos'. The same bewilderment was felt by the actors during the rehearsals, which were extended to an unprecedented twenty-one days. Pirandello made a point of attending every day, and Niccodemi admitted that even if his name appeared on the playbills as director, it was the writer who directed. Faced with the sheer incomprehension of the actors, Pirandello was prepared to spend time explaining the theatrical theories behind individual sections, or the motivations of the characters. While for everyone else 'the structures of the play were confused, imprecise and shapeless, he could see them clearly and unmistakably', Niccodemi wrote.

The audience suffered from the same difficulties as the cast, and the first night in Rome, 9 May 1921, is part of the history of European theatre, but not in any sense that brought comfort to the unfortunate author. The

[1] Dario Niccodemi, *Tempo Passato* (Milan, Treves, 1929), pp. 78–88.

performance ended in a riot. Apparently the audience was restrained at the end of the first two sections of the play, but a torrent of booing broke out at the end of the performance, and an ugly crowd gathered outside the theatre waiting for the playwright to come out. Pirandello conducted himself with dignity, as one friendly eye-witness reported:

> At midnight, he wanted to return home, avoiding if possible the mob, who had insulted him in the theatre with the plebeian, anti-Pirandellist yells – madhouse! [. . .] It was advisable to go out by a side-entrance on to the alley, a dirty alleyway full of dead cats.
>
> He went out with his daughter on his arm. He was recognised as soon as he stepped under a lamp-post. People gathered round to defend him. Beautiful women, with painted lips, jeered and repeated: madhouse! Elegant young men with white ties sneered and shouted insults [. . .] Even the local police did not know whether to intervene in favour of 'that madman, Pirandello'. A taxi approached. Pirandello, in the light of the little piazza, faced the insults head on, with the glimmer of an ironic smile just visible on his lips [. . .] The elegant young men threw coins at him. So too did the ladies, opening their delicate little handbags. I can still hear the copper falling on the pavement, the laughter and the jeers.[1]

The uproar was widely reported, and the play itself reviewed and analysed in all the major newspapers and periodicals in Italy and abroad. Many of these articles were by the major critics and writers of the day, and even those which were broadly in favour still expressed deep and often perceptive criticisms. Adriano Tilgher wrote a long, thoughtful review where appreciation was mixed with criticism. His main points of criticism were that Pirandello allowed the suspense to drop by giving away too much of his plot early on, and that in spite of his stated intentions, by the second act the characters seemed indistinguishable

[1] Orio Vergani, in *Corriere della Sera*, 15 December 1936.

from the human beings.[1] For all his frequently expressed contempt for critics – some of whom found themselves mercilessly ridiculed in his plays – Pirandello seems to have taken note of their comments. However, no changes were made when the script was sent to the publisher, but the opportunity for audiences to familiarise themselves with its novelty helped prepare the way for the next production in Milan on 27 September that same year. This time the play met with general, if still baffled, approval.

By now, Pirandello's fame was international. George Bernard Shaw, to whom many Italian critics compared Pirandello, was favourably impressed and arranged for an English translation, by Edward Storer, and production by the English Stage Society. However, censorship was still in force in Britain, and the Lord Chamberlain stepped in to ban all public performances of the work. His reasoning is bound to seem quaint and curious today. Family values were not upheld adequately, and the depiction of sexuality even inside the family was, in the judgement of the guardian of public morality, altogether too strong meat for tender British stomachs. 'To base a scene upon the horror of a boy seeing his father and mother in a sexual relationship disgusts me and I assume it would sicken and disgust a normal audience,' he intoned.[2] (This suggestion of voyeurism is more explicit in the 1921 version than in the 1925 one.) It can, then, hardly be surprising if the suggestion of incest in the relationship between the Father and the Stepdaughter was viewed by Lord Cromer, the then holder of the office, as altogether beyond the pale. 'No amount of supposed unreality [. . .] can disguise the objectionable fact that a stepfather goes to a brothel, that he nearly has intercourse with his own stepdaughter; that he is saved from this repulsive act by his maltreated wife.' He concluded that 'the core of the play deals with a

[1] The review is included in Basnett and Lorch, pp. 62–5.
[2] Nicholas de Jongh, *Politics, Prudery and Perversion* (London, Methuen, 2000), pp. 67–8.

subject that is quite unpleasant', which may well be true, but begs all the important questions about the role of theatre as an arena for the discussion of even the unpleasant side of life. There was no point in attempting to make the authorities grasp the subtle but basic fact that the event to which they so strenuously objected was supposed not to have taken place, but belonged to a dimension of fiction which was being contrasted with lived reality. The matter was clinched by a Squire Bancroft, a consultant of the Lord Chamberlain, who wrote from the Athenaeum Club in London that Pirandello's play 'is plain filthiness'. His information was not accurate since he added, with what passes for wit among the patrician classes, 'the play I think comes from Vienna. The sooner it goes back there the better.'

In fact, the play stayed in London. By a quirk of English law, a dramatic work judged too subversive or pernicious to be performed in public could be shown in a venue constituted, or reconstituted, as a club. The play was put on by the Stage Society in February 1922 for members only, and was reviewed respectfully in the press. Faced with international derision, the Lord Chamberlain reversed his decision in 1928. In the same year as the British première, an American production was mounted in New York at the Fulton Theatre, renamed the 'Pirandello Theatre' for the duration of a festival of the playwright's drama.

The most significant foreign production of those years was the production in Paris in 1923 by the Georgian-born director, Georges Pitoëff. Pirandello went to France to see the play, and was initially horrified by Pitoëff's use of an on-stage lift to lower the characters from some ethereal, mysterious area down to the terrestrial theatre where the fictional company was rehearsing. He was later reconciled to this innovation. The following year, perhaps the greatest European director of the age, Max Reinhardt, staged the work in Berlin. Pirandello had reservations over the production, but was impressed by Reinhardt's decision to have the characters on stage but in shadow from the beginning. Lighting effects were used to draw the audience's attention to them when it was time for them to make their entrances. Some critics have wondered about Pirandello's real view of Reinhardt, especially since in a later play, *Tonight We Improvise* (1928), he satirised the pretentiousness of a director to whom he gave a German name, Dr Hinkfuss. On the other hand, that work was dedicated to Reinhardt in recognition of his 'unequalled creative power [which] had given magical life to *Six Characters in Search of an Author* on the German stage'.

The early twenties were highly fertile years for Pirandello but he was not able to leave *Six Characters* and move on. He rewrote the play, introducing substantial modifications, for a new published edition in 1924. This was the script he used for a production directed by himself for his new company, the Teatro d'Arte, in May 1925. Other playwrights, notably G. B. Shaw, were in the habit of writing lengthy introductions to explain the reasoning behind their plays, and although Pirandello had not done so previously, he wrote for this new version a Preface which is also one of the most important statements of the semi-philosophy which had become known as *Pirandellismo*. There were other editions and other productions in Pirandello's lifetime, but the 1925 edition, which is used here, can be regarded as the definitive form of the play.

There were many changes between the two versions, although none which affected the 'philosophy' or (as we prefer to call it) the outlook inherent in the play. He extended substantially the 'stage directions' to make them less like hints for movements, entrances and exits, and more like the descriptions and discussions of character which are a feature of the short story. Pirandello did not view theatre as a collaborative exercise, and was prone to viewing the actor as an intrusion between the writer and his public, so the stage directions were a means of direct dialogue with the spectator or reader. The other principal modification is that the 'play-within-a-play' has been much enriched. Space does not permit a list of the many modifications, but it is worth drawing attention to the fact that while in the earlier version, the characters were seemingly inside the theatre and entered from a door at the back of the stage, in the 1925 version they enter from outside and parade down the aisles in the midst of the audience. In addition, perhaps in deference to Tilgher's criticism, he is more insistent on the need to distinguish between the human actors and the invented characters. The mystery, the sense of 'otherness' which envelops them, suggested by lighting, was altogether deeper in the later version. While he did not eliminate it, Pirandello reduced in 1925 the element of abstract reasoning which he allows his characters, the Father in particular. Drama, he had concluded, was essentially action, even if his dialogue continued to lean towards the abstract. Finally the ending is altered. The 1921 version ended with the gunshot and the subsequent screams of 'Fiction! Reality!' from the Father, but in the 1925 version, in keeping with his aim of heightening the other-worldly mystery surrounding the characters, he spread the lines among several characters and ended his play with the haunting, ghostly exit of the Father, Mother and Son and the flight of the Stepdaughter. The final focus is on the drama of the characters to whom he had originally denied life.

*Six Characters* captured, and never lost, a place in the standard canon of recognised European dramatic masterpieces, so that every major theatrical centre has had regular opportunities to see the work staged. The first two post-war productions in Italy, directed in 1946 in Rome by Orazio Costa and in 1953 by Giorgio Strehler in Milan, both used the 1921 script, although this had been superseded by Pirandello's own rewriting. A new production in Rome by Giorgio de Lullo in 1963 aroused hostile comment at the time, not so much for its mingling of the 1921 and 1925 texts as for reducing the atmosphere of arcane mystery surrounding the characters and heightening the profile of the actors by adding extraneous stage business which drew attention to them at points when they should have been no more than bystanders. In the same year, there was a production at the Mayfair Theatre, London, with Sir Ralph Richardson as the Father.

The Royal National Theatre mounted a major production, directed by Michael Rudman, in 1987, with Richard Pasco as the Father and Ralph Fiennes as the Producer. The setting was vaguely Victorian, the age of the actor-manager, but although the acting was generally admired, some critics saw this time-frame as adding an unnecessary extra barrier between performers and audience. In the USA, in 1991, the director-critic Robert Brustein produced an adaptation of his own which his American Repertory Company took to Moscow, where his bold scheme received more praise than it had done at home. The Scottish playwright David Harrower authored what was described as a 'new version', entitled *Six Characters Looking for an Author* (London, Methuen, 2001), staged, under the direction of Richard Jones, by the Old Vic in February 2001. The review in the *Daily Telegraph* carried the headline: 'Putting the shock back into Pirandello'. The Producer, nervously chain-smoking and swallowing pills, led off by giving a lecture with slides on Pirandello's own unhappy life, but his talk was interrupted when the characters erupted through the projection screen on to the stage. The *Telegraph* reviewer, Charles Spencer, judged these innovations favourably for providing a 'fresh perspective on a classic that has been allowed to gather dust'. He described the play itself as 'one of the great works of modernism, as influential as Picasso's cubism or Schoenberg's pioneering work with the twelve-note scale'. The power of *Six Characters in Search of an Author* to intrigue, startle, or even shock, has remained intact over the past eighty years.

# Further Reading

## Selected works by Pirandello in English

*Collected Plays*, ed. Robert Rietty (London, John Calder):
Vol. 1 (1987) contains *Henry IV*, *The Man with the Flower in his Mouth*, *Right You Are! (If You Think So)*, *Lazarus*
Vol. 2 (1988) contains *Six Characters in Search of an Author*, *All for the Best*, *Clothe the Naked*, *Limes from Sicily*
Vol. 3 (1992) contains *The Rules of the Game*, *Each in His Own Way*, *Grafted*, *The Other Son*

*Three Plays*, intro. John Linstrum, contains *The Rules of the Game*, *Six Characters in Search of an Author*, *Henry IV* (London, Methuen, 1988)
*Six Characters Looking for an Author*, version by David Harrower (London, Methuen, 2001)
*Enrico Four*, trans. Robert David Macdonald (London, Oberon Classics, 1996)
*Absolutely! (Perhaps)*, trans. Martin Sherman (London, Methuen, 2003)
*On Humour*, trans. Antonio Illiano and Daniel P. Testa (Chapel Hill, University of North Carolina Press, 1974)
*Pirandello's Love Letters to Marta Abba*, ed. and trans. Benito Ortolani (Princeton, Princeton University Press, 1994)
Preface to *Six Characters in Search of an Author*, trans. Eric Bentley, in *Playwrights on Playwriting*, ed. Toby Cole (New York, Hill and Wang, 1961), pp. 204–17

## Biography

Giudice, Gaspare, *Pirandello: A Biography*, trans. Alastair Hamilton (London, Oxford University Press, 1975)

## Works of criticism on Pirandello

Basnett, Susan and Lorch, Jennifer (eds), *Luigi Pirandello in the Theatre: A Documentary Record* (Reading, Harwood Academic Publishers, 1993)

Basnett-McGuire, Susan, *Luigi Pirandello* (London, Macmillan, 1983)

Bassanese, Fiora A., *Understanding Luigi Pirandello* (Columbia, South Carolina University Press, 1997)

Bloom, Harold (ed.), *Luigi Pirandello* (New York, Chelsea House, 1989)

Budel, Oscar, *Pirandello* (London, Bowes and Bowes, 1966)

Caesar, Ann Hallamore, *Characters and Authors in Luigi Pirandello* (Oxford, Oxford University Press, 1998)

Di Gaetani, John Luis (ed.), *A Companion to Pirandello Studies* (London, Greenwood Press, 1991)

Gunsberg, Maggie, *Patriarchal Representations: Gender and Discourse in Pirandello's Theatre* (Oxford, Berg, 1993)

Matthaei, Renate, *Luigi Pirandello* (New York, Frederick Ungar Publishing Co., 1973)

Ragusa, Olga, *Pirandello: An Approach to His Theatre* (Edinburgh, Edinburgh University Press, 1980)

Vittorini, Domenico, *The Drama of Luigi Pirandello* (Philadelphia, University of Pennsylvania Press, 1935; New York, Russell & Russell, 1969)

*Yearbook of the British Pirandello Society*, annual publication from 1981 onwards

## Books with chapters on Pirandello

Bentley, Eric, *The Life of the Drama* (London, Methuen, 1965)

Bentley, Eric, *The Theatre of War* (London, Eyre Methuen, 1972)

Brustein, Robert, *Theatre of Revolt* (London, Methuen & Co., 1965)

Fergusson, Francis, *The Idea of a Theater* (Princeton, Princeton University Press, 1977)

Szondi, Peter, *Theory of the Modern Drama* (Minneapolis, University of Minneapolis Press, 1987)
Vittorini, Domenico, *High Points in the History of Italian Literature* (New York, David McKay Co., 1958)
Williams, Raymond, *Modern Tragedy* (London, Verso, 1979)

# Translator's Note

Time acts upon a translation in a way that it does not upon the original, so that a translation made a quarter of a century ago might be almost as distant from us as the original itself and in criticising the effectiveness of the play we may find ourselves judging and reacting to a translation and not the work that is translated. The modernisation of a translation is not only acceptable but necessary in order to preserve a sense of freshness as language itself changes. An original work possesses a natural elasticity of language that allows it to accommodate these changes more easily than a translation which is inevitably limited by attempts to be both lucid and faithful to an original.

My aim has been to offer an accurate, new translation that sensitively adjusts the language to suit a new age of audience, not to tamper with the quality and form of the play or to offer a totally restructured version. Above all, I hope to have given actors who perform the play lines to speak that they find entirely appropriate and comfortable.

This play is of some importance in the development of the theatre of the twentieth century and deserves better than to be relegated to the status of a period-piece: in 1921, when the play was first performed, it was far ahead of its time, not only in its form but because the central thought was so original and astonishing. Imagined but uncompleted characters burst into reality from an author's creative mind with an explosive, dynamic power; that is both a startling and a timeless event. However, despite its ageless theme, embedded in this remarkable play there are factors that compel us to leave it in a period rather earlier than today. If we show the Actors in jeans, jerseys, modern jewellery, the fashionable undress of today, we shall also have to give them a style of language and behaviour to match and this would be destructive of the relationship that Pirandello needed between the Characters and the Actors. The details of the family life of the Characters with its disruption, adultery, prostitution, illegitimacy, nudity and potential incest would be reduced in their effectiveness in a late twentieth-century setting. With that in mind I have retained the title Producer and Prompter rather than change them to Director and DSM as in current theatrical practice. The older forms suggest a theatrical hierarchy which is no longer so obvious but which is contained in the attitudes of the people in the play. It would be tempting to compose a totally new version in which the framework, the style and the language are altered, but that would be to rewrite the play not translate it, and it would, I suspect, lose more than it gained.

John Linstrum
Penarth, 1984

# Six Characters in Search of an Author

*translated by John Linstrum*

**The Characters:**

**The Father**
**The Mother**
**The Stepdaughter**
**The Son**
**The Boy** (*non-speaking*)
**The Little Girl** (*non-speaking*)
**Madame Pace**

**The Actors:**

**The Producer**
**The Leading Actress**
**The Leading Actor**
**The Second Actress**
**The Young Actress**
**The Young Actor**
**Other actors and actresses** (*a variable number*)
**The Stage Manager**
**The Prompter**
**The Property Man**
**The Stage-hand**
**The Producer's Secretary**
**The Doorkeeper**
**Other theatre staff**

The action of the play takes place on the stage of a theatre. There are no act or scene divisions, but there are two interruptions: when the Producer and the Characters go to the office to write the scenario, giving the Actors a break in rehearsal, and when a stage-hand lowers the front curtain by mistake.

*References to 'prompt-box', 'curtains' and 'letting down trees' will need to be altered if they are not appropriate to the theatre where the performance is taking place.*

This translation was first presented at the Greenwich Theatre, London, in June 1979, with the following cast:

**The Characters:**

| | |
|---|---|
| **The Father** | Philip Stone |
| **The Mother** | Mona Bruce |
| **The Stepdaughter** | Pauline Moran |
| **The Son** | Nick Dunning |
| **The Boy** | Stuart Wilde |
| **The Little Girl** | Clare Barnes/<br>Charlotte Levitt/<br>Rachel Quarmby |
| **Madame Pace** | Claire Davenport |

**The Company:**

| | |
|---|---|
| **The Producer** | Michael Jackson |
| **Stage staff** | Deborah Blake<br>Jeannie Crowther<br>Mark Preston |
| **The Actors** | David Beale<br>Sally Nesbitt<br>Christopher Saul<br>Erica Stevens<br>Joanna Wake |

*Directed by* Phil Young
*Designed by* Bernard Culshaw

# Act One

*When the audience enters, the curtain is already up and the stage is just as it would be during the day. There is no set; it is empty, in almost total darkness. This is so that from the beginning the audience will have the feeling of being present, not at a performance of a properly rehearsed play, but at a performance of a play that happens spontaneously. Two small sets of steps, one on the right and one on the left, lead up to the stage from the auditorium. On the stage, the top is off the* **Prompter***'s box and is lying next to it. Downstage, there is a small table and a chair with arms for the* **Producer***: it is turned with its back to the audience.*

*Also downstage there are two small tables, one a little bigger than the other, and several chairs, ready for the rehearsal if needed. There are more chairs scattered on both left and right for the* **Actors***: to one side at the back and nearly hidden is a piano.*

*When the houselights go down the* **Stage-hand** *comes on through the back door. He is in blue overalls and carries a tool bag. He brings some pieces of wood on, comes to the front, kneels down and starts to nail them together.*

*The* **Stage Manager** *rushes on from the wings.*

**Stage Manager** Hey! What are you doing?

**Stage-hand** What do you think I'm doing? I'm banging nails in.

**Stage Manager** Now? (*He looks at his watch.*) It's half-past ten already. The Producer will be here in a moment to rehearse.

**Stage-hand** I've got to do my work some time, you know.

**Stage Manager** Right – but not now.

**Stage-hand** When?

**Stage Manager** When the rehearsal's finished. Come

on, get all this out of the way and let me set for the second act of *The Rules of the Game.*

*The* **Stage-hand** *picks up his tools and wood and goes off, grumbling and muttering. The* **Actors** *of the company come in through the door, men and women, first one, then another, then two together and so on: there will be nine or ten, enough for the parts for the rehearsal of a play by Pirandello,* The Rules of the Game, *today's rehearsal. They come in, say their 'Good-mornings' to the* **Stage Manager** *and each other. Some go off to the dressing-rooms; others, among them the* **Prompter** *with the text rolled up under his arm, scatter about the stage waiting for the* **Producer** *to start the rehearsal. Meanwhile, sitting or standing in groups, they chat together; some smoke, one complains about his part, another one loudly reads something from* The Stage. *It would be as well if the* **Actors** *and* **Actresses** *were dressed in colourful clothes, and this first scene should be improvised naturally and vivaciously. After a while somebody might sit down at the piano and play a song; the younger* **Actors** *and* **Actresses** *start dancing.*

**Stage Manager** (*clapping his hands to call their attention*) Come on everybody! Quiet please. The Producer's here.

*The piano and the dancing both stop. The* **Actors** *turn to look out into the theatre and through the door at the back comes the* **Producer**. *He walks down the gangway between the seats and, calling 'Good-morning' to the* **Actors**, *climbs up one of the sets of stairs on to the stage. The* **Secretary** *gives him the post, a few magazines, a script. The* **Actors** *move to one side of the stage.*

**Producer** Any letters?

**Secretary** No. That's all the post there is. (*Giving him the script.*)

**Producer** Put it in the office. (*Then looking round and turning to the* **Stage Manager**.) I can't see a thing here. Let's have some lights please.

**Stage Manager** Right. (*Calling.*) Workers please!

*In a few seconds the side of the stage where the* **Actors** *are standing* *is brilliantly lit with white light. The* **Prompter** *has gone into his box and spread out his script.*

**Producer** Good. (*Clapping hands.*) Well then, let's get started. Anybody missing?

**Stage Manager** (*heavily ironic*) Our leading lady.

**Producer** Not again! (*Looking at his watch.*) We're ten minutes late already. Send her a note to come and see me. It might teach her to be on time for rehearsals. (*Almost before he has finished, the* **Leading Actress***'s voice is heard from the auditorium.*)

**Leading Actress** Morning everybody. Sorry I'm late. (*She is very expensively dressed and is carrying a lap-dog. She comes down the aisle and goes up on to the stage.*)

**Producer** You're determined to keep us waiting, aren't you?

**Leading Actress** I'm sorry. I just couldn't find a taxi anywhere. But you haven't started yet and I'm not on at the opening anyhow. (*Calling the* **Stage Manager**, *she gives him the dog.*) Put him in my dressing-room for me will you?

**Producer** And she's even brought her lap-dog with her! As if we haven't enough lap-dogs here already. (*Clapping his hands and turning to the* **Prompter**.) Right then, the second act of *The Rules of the Game*. (*Sits in his armchair.*) Quiet please! Who's on?

*The* **Actors** *clear from the front of the stage and sit to one side, except for three who are ready to start the scene and the* **Leading Actress**. *She has ignored the* **Producer** *and is sitting at one of the little tables.*

**Producer** Are you in this scene, then?

**Leading Actress** No – I've just told you.

**Producer** (*annoyed*) Then get off, for God's sake. (*The* **Leading Actress** *goes and sits with the others. To the* **Prompter**.) Come on then, let's get going.

**Prompter** (*reading his script*) 'The house of Leone Gala. A peculiar room, both dining-room and study.'

**Producer** (*to the* **Stage Manager**) We'll use the red set.

**Stage Manager** (*making a note*) The red set – right.

**Prompter** (*still reading*) 'The table is laid and there is a desk with books and papers. Bookcases full of books and china cabinets full of valuable china. An exit at the back leads to Leone's bedroom. An exit to the left leads to the kitchen. The main entrance is on the right.'

**Producer** Right. Listen carefully everybody: there, the main entrance, there, the kitchen. (*To the* **Leading Actor** *who plays Socrates.*) Your entrances and exits will be from there. (*To the* **Stage Manager**.) We'll have the french windows there and put the curtains on them.

**Stage Manager** (*making a note*) Right.

**Prompter** (*reading*) 'Scene One. Leone Gala, Guido Venanzi, and Filippo, who is called Socrates.' (*To* **Producer**.) Have I to read the directions as well?

**Producer** Yes, you have! I've told you a hundred times.

**Prompter** (*reading*) 'When the curtain rises, Leone Gala, in a cook's hat and apron, is beating an egg in a dish with a little wooden spoon. Filippo is beating another and he is dressed as a cook too. Guido Venanzi is sitting listening.'

**Leading Actor** Look, do I really have to wear a cook's hat?

**Producer** (*annoyed by the question*) I expect so! That's what it says in the script. (*Pointing to the script.*)

**Leading Actor** If you ask me it's ridiculous.

**Producer** (*leaping to his feet furiously*) Ridiculous? It's ridiculous, is it? What do you expect me to do if nobody writes good plays any more and we're reduced to putting on plays by Pirandello? And if you can understand them you must be very clever. He writes them on purpose so nobody enjoys them, neither actors nor critics nor audience. (*The* **Actors** *laugh. He then crosses to* **Leading Actor** *and shouts at him.*) A cook's hat and you beat eggs. But don't run away with the idea that that's all you are doing – beating eggs. You must be joking! You have to be symbolic of the shells of the eggs you are beating. (*The* **Actors** *laugh again and start making ironical comments to each other.*) Be quiet! Listen carefully while I explain. (*Turns back to* **Leading Actor**.) Yes, the shells, because they are symbolic of the empty form of reason, without its content, blind instinct! You are reason and your wife is instinct: you are playing a game where you have been given parts and in which you are not just yourself but the puppet of yourself. Do you see?

**Leading Actor** (*spreading his hands*) Me? No.

**Producer** (*going back to his chair*) Neither do I! Come on, let's get going; you wait till you see the end! You haven't seen anything yet! (*Confidentially.*) By the way, I should turn almost to face the audience if I were you, about three-quarters face. Well, what with the obscure dialogue and the audience not being able to hear you properly in any case, the whole lot'll go to hell. (*Clapping hands again.*) Come on. Let's get going!

**Prompter** Excuse me, can I put the top back on the prompt-box? There's a bit of a draught.

**Producer** Yes, yes, of course. Get on with it.

*The* **Stage Doorkeeper**, *in a braided cap, has come into the auditorium, and he comes all the way down the aisle to the stage to tell the* **Producer** *the* **Six Characters** *have come, who, having come in after him, look about them a little puzzled and dismayed. Every effort must be made to create the effect that the* **Six Characters** *are very different from the* **Actors** *of the company. The placings of the two groups, indicated in the directions, once the* **Characters** *are on the stage, will help this; so will using different coloured lights. But the most effective idea is to use masks for the*

**Characters**, *masks specially made of a material that will not go limp with perspiration and light enough not to worry the actors who wear them: they should be made so that the eyes, the nose and the mouth are all free. This is the way to bring out the deep significance of the play. The* **Characters** *should not appear as ghosts, but as created realities, timeless creations of the imagination, and so more real and consistent than the changeable realities of the* **Actors**. *The masks are designed to give the impression of figures constructed by art, each one fixed for ever in its own fundamental emotion; that is, Remorse for the* **Father**, *Revenge for the* **Stepdaughter**, *Scorn for the* **Son**, *Sorrow for the* **Mother**. *Her mask should have wax tears in the corners of the eyes and down the cheeks like the sculptured or painted weeping Madonna in a church. Her dress should be of a plain material, in stiff folds, looking almost as if it were carved and not of an ordinary material you can buy in a shop and have made up by a dressmaker.*

*The* **Father** *is about fifty: his reddish hair is thinning at the temples, but he is not bald: he has a full moustache that almost covers his young-looking mouth, which often opens in an uncertain and empty smile. He is pale, with a high forehead: he has blue oval eyes, clear and sharp: he is dressed in light trousers and a dark jacket: his voice is sometimes rich, at other times harsh and loud.*

*The* **Mother** *appears crushed by an intolerable weight of shame and humiliation. She is wearing a thick black veil and is dressed simply in black; when she raises her veil she shows a face like wax, but not suffering, with her eyes turned down humbly.*

*The* **Stepdaughter**, *who is eighteen years old, is defiant, even insolent. She is very beautiful, dressed in mourning as well, but with striking elegance. She is scornful of the timid, suffering, dejected air of her young brother, a grubby little* **Boy** *of fourteen, also dressed in black; she is full of a warm tenderness, on the other hand, for the little sister, a* **Girl** *of about four, dressed in white with a black silk sash round her waist.*

*The* **Son** *is twenty-two, tall, almost frozen in an air of scorn for the* **Father** *and indifference to the* **Mother**; *he is wearing a mauve overcoat and a long green scarf round his neck.*

**Doorkeeper** Excuse me, sir.

**Producer** (*angrily*) What the hell is it now?

**Doorkeeper** There are some people here – they say they want to see you, sir.

*The* **Producer** *and the* **Actors** *are astonished and turn to look out into the auditorium.*

**Producer** But I'm rehearsing! You know perfectly well that no one's allowed in during rehearsals. (*Turning to face out front.*) Who are you? What do you want?

**Father** (*coming forward, followed by the others, to the foot of one of the sets of steps*) We're looking for an author.

**Producer** (*angry and astonished*) An author? Which author?

**Father** Any author will do, sir.

**Producer** But there isn't an author here because we're not rehearsing a new play.

**Stepdaughter** (*excitedly as she rushes up the steps*) That's better still, better still! We can be your new play.

**Actors** (*lively comments and laughter from the* **Actors**) Oh, listen to that, *etc.*

**Father** (*going up on the stage after the* **Stepdaughter**) Maybe, but if there isn't an author here . . . (*To the* **Producer**.) Unless you'd like to be . . .

*Hand in hand, the* **Mother** *and the* **Little Girl**, *followed by the* **Little Boy**, *go up on the stage and wait. The* **Son** *stays sullenly behind.*

**Producer** Is this some kind of joke?

**Father** Now, how can you think that? On the contrary, we are bringing you a story of anguish.

**Stepdaughter** We might make your fortune for you!

**Producer** Do me a favour, will you? Go away. We

haven't time to waste on idiots.

**Father** (*hurt but answering gently*) You know very well, as a man of the theatre, that life is full of all sorts of odd things which have no need at all to pretend to be real because they are actually true.

**Producer** What the devil are you talking about?

**Father** What I'm saying is that you really must be mad to do things the opposite way round: to create situations that obviously aren't true and try to make them seem to be really happening. But then I suppose that sort of madness is the only reason for your profession.

*The* **Actors** *are indignant.*

**Producer** (*getting up and glaring at him*) Oh, yes? So ours is a profession of madmen, is it?

**Father** Well, if you try to make something look true when it obviously isn't, especially if you're not forced to do it, but do it for a game . . . Isn't it your job to give life on the stage to imaginary people?

**Producer** (*quickly answering him and speaking for the* **Actors** *who are growing more indignant*) I should like you to know, sir, that the actor's profession is one of great distinction. Even if nowadays the new writers only give us dull plays to act and puppets to present instead of men, I'd have you know that it is our boast that we have given life, here on this stage, to immortal works.

*The* **Actors**, *satisfied, agree with and applaud the* **Producer**.

**Father** (*cutting in and following hard on his argument*) There! You see? Good! You've given life! You've created living beings with more genuine life than people have who breathe and wear clothes! Less real, perhaps, but nearer the truth. We are both saying the same thing.

*The* **Actors** *look at each other, astonished.*

**Producer** But just a moment! You said before . . .

**Father** I'm sorry, but I said that before, about acting for fun, because you shouted at us and said you'd no time to waste on idiots, but you must know better than anyone that Nature uses human imagination to lift her work of creation to even higher levels.

**Producer** All right then: but where does all this get us?

**Father** Nowhere. I want to try to show that one can be thrust into life in many ways, in many forms: as a tree or a stone, as water or a butterfly – or as a woman. It might even be as a character in a play.

**Producer** (*ironic, pretending to be annoyed*) And you, and these other people here, were thrust into life, as you put it, as characters in a play?

**Father** Exactly! And alive, as you can see.

*The* **Producer** *and the* **Actors** *burst into laughter as if at a joke.*

**Father** I'm sorry you laugh like that, because we carry in us, as I said before, a story of terrible anguish as you can guess from this woman dressed in black.

*Saying this, he offers his hand to the* **Mother** *and helps her up the last steps and, holding her still by the hand, leads her with a sense of tragic solemnity across the stage which is suddenly lit by a fantastic light.*

*The* **Little Girl** *and the* **Boy** *follow the* **Mother**: *then the* **Son** *comes up and stands to one side in the background: then the* **Stepdaughter** *follows and leans against the proscenium arch: the* **Actors** *are astonished at first, but then, full of admiration for the 'entrance', they burst into applause – just as if it were a performance specially for them.*

**Producer** (*at first astonished and then indignant*) My God! Be quiet all of you. (*Turns to the* **Characters**.) And you lot get out! Clear off! (*To the* **Stage Manager**.) Jesus! Get them out of here.

**Stage Manager** (*comes forward but stops short as if held back by* *something strange)* Go on out! Get out!

**Father** (*to* **Producer**) Oh no, please, you see, we . . .

**Producer** (*shouting*) We came here to work, you know.

**Leading Actor** We really can't be messed about like this.

**Father** (*resolutely, coming forward*) I'm astonished! Why don't you believe me? Perhaps you are not used to seeing the characters created by an author spring into life up here on the stage face to face with each other. Perhaps it's because we're not in a script? (*He points to the* **Prompter***'s box.*)

**Stepdaughter** (*coming down to the* **Producer**, *smiling and persuasive*) Believe me, sir, we really are six of the most fascinating characters. But we've been neglected.

**Father** Yes, that's right, we've been neglected. In the sense that the author who created us, living in his mind, wouldn't or couldn't make us live in a written play for the world of art. And that really is a crime, sir, because whoever has the luck to be born a character can laugh even at death. Because a character will never die! A man will die, a writer, the instrument of creation: but what he has created will never die! And to be able to live for ever you don't need to have extraordinary gifts or be able to do miracles. Who was Sancho Panza? Who was Prospero? But they will live for ever because – living seeds – they had the luck to find a fruitful soil, an imagination which knew how to grow them and feed them, so that they will live for ever.

**Producer** This is all very well! But what do you want here?

**Father** We want to live, sir.

**Producer** (*ironically*) For ever!

**Father** No, no: only for a few moments – in you.

**An Actor** Listen to that!

**Leading Actress** They want to live in us!

**Young Actor** (*pointing to the* **Stepdaughter**) I don't mind . . . so long as I get her.

**Father** Listen, listen: the play is all ready to be put together and if you and your actors would like to, we can work it out now between us.

**Producer** (*annoyed*) But what exactly do you want to do? We don't make up plays like that here! We present comedies and tragedies here.

**Father** That's right, we know that of course. That's why we've come.

**Producer** And where's the script?

**Father** It's in us, sir. (*The* **Actors** *laugh.*) The play is in us: we are the play and we are impatient to show it to you: the passion inside us is driving us on.

**Stepdaughter** (*scornfully, with the tantalising charm of deliberate impudence*) My passion, if only you knew! My passion for him! (*She points at the* **Father** *and suggests that she is going to embrace him: but stops and bursts into a screeching laugh.*)

**Father** (*with sudden anger*) You keep out of this for the moment! And stop laughing like that!

**Stepdaughter** Really? Then with your permission, ladies and gentlemen; even though it's only two months since I became an orphan, just watch how I can sing and dance.

*The* **Actors**, *especially the younger, seem strangely attracted to her while she sings and dances and they edge closer and reach out their hands to catch hold of her.*[1] *She eludes them, and when the* **Actors** *applaud her and the* **Producer** *speaks sharply to her she stays still quite removed from them all.*

[1] Suggested songs: Eartha Kitt's 'Old Fashioned Millionaire'; theme song from *The Moon is Blue*; 'I'm Gonna Wash That Man Right Out Of My Hair' from *South Pacific*.

**Actor 1** Very good! *etc.*

**Producer** (*angrily*) Be quiet! Do you think this is a night-club? (*Turns to* **Father** *and asks with some concern.*) Is she a bit mad?

**Father** Mad? Oh no – it's worse than that.

**Stepdaughter** (*suddenly running to the* **Producer**) Yes. It's worse, much worse! Listen please! Let's put this play on at once, because you'll see that at a particular point I – when this darling little girl here – (*Taking the* **Little Girl** *by the hand from next to the* **Mother** *and crossing with her to the* **Producer**.) Isn't she pretty? (*Takes her in her arms.*) Darling! Darling! (*Puts her down again and adds, moved very deeply but almost without wanting to.*) Well, this lovely little girl here, when God suddenly takes her from this poor mother: and this little idiot here (*Turning to the* **Little Boy** *and seizing him roughly by the sleeve.*) does the most stupid thing, like the half-wit he is, – then you will see me run away! Yes, you'll see me rush away! But not yet, not yet! Because, after all the intimate things there have been between him and me (*In the direction of the* **Father**, *with a horrible vulgar wink.*) I can't stay with them any longer, to watch the insult to this mother through that supercilious cretin over there. (*Pointing to the* **Son**.) Look at him! Look at him! Condescending, stand-offish, because he's the legitimate son, him! Full of contempt for me, for the boy and for the little girl: because we are bastards. Do you understand? Bastards. (*Running to the* **Mother** *and embracing her.*) And this poor mother – she – who is the mother of all of us – he doesn't want to recognise her as his own mother – and he looks down on her, he does, as if she were only the mother of the three of us who are bastards – the traitor. (*She says all this quickly, with great excitement, and after having raised her voice on the word 'bastards' she speaks quietly, half-spitting the word 'traitor'.*)

**Mother** (*with deep anguish to the* **Producer**) Sir, in the name of these two little ones, I beg you . . . (*Feels herself grow faint and sways.*) Oh, my God.

**Father** (*rushing to support her with almost all the* **Actors** *bewildered and concerned*) Get a chair someone . . . quick, get a chair for this poor widow.

*One of the* **Actors** *offers a chair: the others press urgently around. The* **Mother**, *seated now, tries to stop the* **Father** *lifting her veil.*

**Actors** Is it real? Has she really fainted? *etc.*

**Father** Look at her, everybody, look at her.

**Mother** No, for God's sake, stop it.

**Father** Let them look!

**Mother** (*lifting her hands and covering her face, desperately*) Oh, please, I beg you, stop him from doing what he is trying to do; it's hateful.

**Producer** (*overwhelmed, astounded*) It's no use, I don't understand this any more. (*To the* **Father**.) Is this woman your wife?

**Father** (*at once*) That's right, she is my wife.

**Producer** How is she a widow, then, if you're still alive?

*The* **Actors** *are bewildered too and find relief in a loud laugh.*

**Father** (*wounded, with rising resentment*) Don't laugh! Please don't laugh like that! That's just the point, that's her own drama. You see, she had another man. Another man who ought to be here.

**Mother** No, no! (*Crying out.*)

**Stepdaughter** Luckily for him he died. Two months ago, as I told you: we are in mourning for him, as you can see.

**Father** Yes, he's dead: but that's not the reason he isn't here. He isn't here because – well just look at her, please, and you'll understand at once – hers is not a passionate drama of the love of two men, because she was incapable of love, she could feel nothing – except, perhaps a little gratitude (but not to me, to him). She's not a woman; she's a mother. And her drama – and, believe me, it's a powerful one – her drama is focused completely on these four children of the two men she had.

**Mother** I had them? How dare you say that I had them, as if I wanted them myself? It was him, sir! He forced the other man on me. He made me go away with him!

**Stepdaughter** (*leaping up, indignantly*) It isn't true!

**Mother** (*bewildered*) How isn't it true?

**Stepdaughter** It isn't true, it just isn't true.

**Mother** What do you know about it?

**Stepdaughter** It isn't true. (*To the* **Producer**.) Don't believe it! Do you know why she said that? She said it because of him, over there. (*Pointing to the* **Son**.) She tortures herself, she exhausts herself with worry and all because of the indifference of that son of hers. She wants to make him believe that she abandoned him when he was two years old because the father made her do it.

**Mother** (*passionately*) He did! He made me! God's my witness. (*To the* **Producer**.) Ask him if it isn't true. (*Pointing to the* **Father**.) Make him tell our son it's true. (*Turning to the* **Stepdaughter**.) You don't know anything about it.

**Stepdaughter** I know that when my father was alive you were always happy and contented. You can't deny it.

**Mother** No, I can't deny it.

**Stepdaughter** He was always full of love and care for you. (*Turning to the* **Little Boy** *with anger*.) Isn't it true? Admit it. Why don't you say something, you little idiot?

**Mother** Leave the poor boy alone! Why do you want to make me appear ungrateful? You're my daughter. I don't in the least want to offend your father's memory. I've already told him that it wasn't my fault or even to please myself that I left his house and my son.

**Father** It's quite true. It was my fault.

**Leading Actor** (*to other actors*) Look at this. What a show!

**Leading Actress** And we're the audience.

**Young Actor** For a change.

**Producer** (*beginning to be very interested*) Let's listen to them! Quiet! Listen!

*He goes down the steps into the auditorium and stands there as if to get an idea of what the scene will look like from the audience's viewpoint.*

**Son** (*without moving, coldly, quietly, ironically*) Yes, listen to his little scrap of philosophy. He's going to tell you all about the Daemon of Experiment.

**Father** You're a cynical idiot, and I've told you so a hundred times. (*To the* **Producer** *who is now in the stalls.*) He sneers at me because of this expression I've found to defend myself.

**Son** Words, words.

**Father** Yes words, words! When we're faced by something we don't understand, by a sense of evil that seems as if it's going to swallow us, don't we all find comfort in a word that tells us nothing but that calms us?

**Stepdaughter** And dulls your sense of remorse, too. That more than anything.

**Father** Remorse? No, that's not true. It'd take more than words to dull the sense of remorse in me.

**Stepdaughter** It's taken a little money too, just a little money. The money that he was going to offer as payment, gentlemen.

*The* **Actors** *are horrified.*

**Son** (*contemptuously to his stepsister*) That's a filthy trick.

**Stepdaughter** A filthy trick? There it was in a pale blue envelope on the little mahogany table in the room behind the shop at Madame Pace's. You know Madame Pace, don't you? One of those Madames who sell 'Robes et Manteaux' so that they can attract poor girls like me from decent families into their workroom.

**Son** And she's bought the right to tyrannise over the whole lot of us with that money – with what he was going to pay her: and luckily – now listen carefully – he had no reason to pay it to her.

**Stepdaughter** But it was close!

**Mother** (*rising up angrily*) Shame on you, daughter! Shame!

**Stepdaughter** Shame? Not shame, revenge! I'm desperate, desperate to live that scene! The room . . . over here the showcase of coats, there the divan, there the mirror, and the screen, and over there in front of the window, that little mahogany table with the pale blue envelope and the money in it. I can see it all quite clearly. I could pick it up! But you should turn your faces away, gentlemen: because I'm nearly naked! I'm not blushing any longer – I leave that to him. (*Pointing at the* **Father**.) But I tell you he was very pale, very pale then. (*To the* **Producer**.) Believe me.

**Producer** I don't understand any more.

**Father** I'm not surprised when you're attacked like that! Why don't you put your foot down and let me have my say before you believe all these horrible slanders she's so viciously telling about me.

**Stepdaughter** We don't want to hear any of your long-winded fairy-stories.

**Father** I'm not going to tell any fairy-stories! I want to explain things to him.

**Stepdaughter** I'm sure you do. Oh, yes! In your own special way.

*The* **Producer** *comes back up on stage to take control.*

**Father** But isn't that the cause of all the trouble? Words! We all have a world of things inside ourselves and each one of us has his own private world. How can we understand each other if the words I use have the sense and the value that I expect them to have, but whoever is listening to me inevitably thinks that those same words have a different sense and value, because of the private world he has inside himself too. We think we understand each other: but we never do. Look! All my pity, all my compassion for this woman (*Pointing to the* **Mother**.) she sees as ferocious cruelty.

**Mother** But he turned me out of the house!

**Father** There, do you hear? I turned her out! She really believed that I had turned her out.

**Mother** You know how to talk. I don't . . . But believe me, sir, (*Turning to the* **Producer**.) after he married me . . . I can't think why! I was a poor, simple woman.

**Father** But that was the reason! I married you for your simplicity, that's what I loved in you, believing – (*He stops because she is making gestures of contradiction. Then, seeing the impossibility of making her understand, he throws his arms wide in a gesture of desperation and turns back to the* **Producer**.) No, do you see? She says no! It's terrifying, sir, believe me, terrifying, her deafness, her mental deafness. (*He taps his forehead.*) Affection for her children, oh yes. But deaf, mentally deaf, deaf, sir, to the point of desperation.

**Stepdaughter** Yes, but make him tell you what good all his cleverness has brought us.

**Father** If only we could see in advance all the harm that can come from the good we think we are doing.

*The* **Leading Actress**, *who has been growing angry watching the* **Leading Actor** *flirting with the* **Stepdaughter**, *comes forward and snaps at the* **Producer**.

**Leading Actress** Excuse me, are we going to go on with our rehearsal?

**Producer** Yes, of course. But I want to listen to this first.

**Young Actor** It's such a new idea.

**Young Actress** It's fascinating.

**Leading Actress** For those who are interested. (*She looks meaningfully at the* **Leading Actor**.)

**Producer** (*to the* **Father**) Look here, you must explain yourself more clearly. (*He sits down.*)

**Father** Listen then. You see, there was a rather poor fellow working for me as my assistant and secretary, very loyal: he understood her in everything. (*Pointing to the* **Mother**.) But without a hint of deceit, you must believe that: he was good and simple, like her: neither of them was capable even of thinking anything wrong, let alone doing it.

**Stepdaughter** So instead he thought of it for them and did it too!

**Father** It's not true! What I did was for their good – oh yes and mine too, I admit it! The time had come when I couldn't say a word to either of them without there immediately flashing between them a sympathetic look: each one caught the other's eye for advice, about how to take what I had said, how not to make me angry. Well, that was enough, as I'm sure you'll understand, to put me in a bad temper all the time, in a state of intolerable exasperation.

**Producer** Then why didn't you sack this secretary of yours?

**Father** Right! In the end I did sack him! But then I had to watch this poor woman wandering about in the house on her own, forlorn, like a stray animal you take in out of pity.

**Mother** It's quite true.

**Father** (*suddenly, turning to her, as if to stop her*) And what about the boy? Is that true as well?

**Mother** But first he tore my son from me, sir.

**Father** But not out of cruelty! It was so that he could grow up healthy and strong, in touch with the earth.

**Stepdaughter** (*pointing to the* **Son** *jeeringly*) And look at the result!

**Father** (*quickly*) And is it my fault, too, that he's grown up like this? I took him to a nurse in the country, a peasant, because his mother didn't seem strong enough to me, although she is from a humble family herself. In fact that was what made me marry her. Perhaps it was superstitious of me; but what was I to do? I've always had this dreadful longing for a kind of sound moral healthiness.

*The* **Stepdaughter** *breaks out again into noisy laughter.*

**Father** Make her stop that! It's unbearable.

**Producer** Stop it will you? Let me listen, for God's sake.

*When the* **Producer** *has spoken to her, she resumes her previous position . . . absorbed and distant, a half-smile on her lips. The* **Producer** *comes down into the auditorium again to see how it looks from there.*

**Father** I couldn't bear the sight of this woman near me. (*Pointing to the* **Mother**.) Not so much because of the annoyance she caused me, you see, or even the feeling of being stifled, being suffocated that I got from her, as for the sorrow, the painful sorrow that I felt for her.

**Mother** And he sent me away.

**Father** With everything you needed, to the other man, to set her free from me.

**Mother** And to set yourself free!

**Father** Oh, yes, I admit it. And what terrible things came out of it. But I did it for the best, and more for her than for me: I swear it! (*Folds his arms: then turns suddenly to the* **Mother**.) I never lost sight of you did I? Until that fellow, without my knowing it, suddenly took you off to another town one day. He was idiotically suspicious of my interest in them, a genuine interest, I assure you, without any ulterior motive at all. I watched the new little family growing up round her with unbelievable tenderness, she'll confirm that. (*He points to the* **Stepdaughter**.)

**Stepdaughter** Oh yes, I can indeed. I was a pretty little girl, you know, with plaits down to my shoulders and my little frilly knickers showing under my dress – so pretty – he used to watch me coming out of school. He came to see how I was maturing.

**Father** That's shameful! It's monstrous.

**Stepdaughter** No it isn't! Why do you say it is?

**Father** It's montrous! Monstrous. (*He turns excitedly to the* **Producer** *and goes on in explanation.*) After she'd gone away (*Pointing to the* **Mother**.), my house seemed empty. She'd been like a weight on my spirit but she'd filled the house with her presence. Alone in the empty rooms I wandered about like a lost soul. This boy here (*Indicating the* **Son**), growing up away from home – whenever he came back to the home – I don't know – but he didn't seem to be mine any more. We needed the mother between us, to link us together, and so he grew up by himself, apart, with no connection to me either through intellect or love. And then – it must seem odd, but it's true – first I was curious about and then strongly attracted to the little family that had come about because of what I'd done. And the thought of them began to fill all the emptiness that I felt around me. I needed, I really needed to believe that she was happy, wrapped up in the simple cares of her life, lucky because she was better off away from the complicated torments of a soul like mine. And to prove it, I used to watch that child coming out of school.

**Stepdaughter** Listen to him! He used to follow me

along the street; he used to smile at me and when we came near the house he'd wave his hand – like this! I watched him, wide-eyed, puzzled. I didn't know who he was. I told my mother about him and she knew at once who it must be. (**Mother** *nods agreement.*) At first, she didn't let me go to school again, at any rate for a few days. But when I did go back, I saw him standing near the door again – looking ridiculous – with a brown paper-bag in his hand. He came close and petted me: then he opened the bag and took out a beautiful straw hat with a hoop of rosebuds round it – for me!

**Producer** All this is off the point, you know.

**Son** (*contemptuously*) Yes . . . literature, literature.

**Father** What do you mean, literature? This is real life: real passions.

**Producer** That may be! But you can't put it on the stage just like that.

**Father** That's right you can't. Because all this is only leading up to the main action. I'm not suggesting that this part should be put on the stage. In any case, you can see for yourself, (*Pointing at the* **Stepdaughter**.) she isn't a pretty little girl any longer with plaits down to her shoulders.

**Stepdaughter** – and with frilly knickers showing under her frock.

**Father** The drama begins now: and it's new and complex.

**Stepdaughter** (*coming forward, fierce and brooding*) As soon as my father died . . .

**Father** (*quickly, not giving her time to speak*) They were so miserable. They came back here, but I didn't know about it because of the Mother's stubbornness. (*Pointing to the* **Mother**.) She can't really write you know; but she could have got her daughter to write, or the boy, to tell me that they needed help.

**Mother** But tell me, sir, how could I have known how he felt?

**Father** And hasn't that always been your fault? You've never known anything about how I felt.

**Mother** After all the years away from him and after all that had happened.

**Father** And was it my fault if that fellow took you so far away? (*Turning back to the* **Producer**.) Suddenly, overnight, I tell you, he'd found a job away from here without my knowing anything about it. I couldn't possibly trace them; and then, naturally I suppose, my interest in them grew less over the years. The drama broke out, unexpected and violent, when they came back: when I was driven in misery by the needs of my flesh, still alive with desire . . . and it is misery, you know, unspeakable misery for the man who lives alone and who detests sordid, casual affairs; not old enough to do without women, but not young enough to be able to go and look for one without shame! Misery? Is that what I called it? It's horrible, it's revolting, because there isn't a woman who will give her love to me any more. And when he realises this, he should do without . . . It's easy to say though. Each of us, face to face with other men, is clothed with some sort of dignity, but we know only too well all the unspeakable things that go on in the heart. We surrender, we give in to temptation: but afterwards we rise up out of it very quickly, in a desperate hurry to rebuild our dignity, whole and firm as if it were a gravestone that would cover every sign and memory of our shame, and hide it from even our own eyes. Everyone's like that, only some of us haven't the courage to talk about it.

**Stepdaughter** But they've all got the courage to do it!

**Father** Yes! But only in secret! That's why it takes more courage to talk about it! Because if a man does talk about it – what happens then? – everybody says he's a cynic.

And it's simply not true; he's just like everybody else; only better perhaps, because he's not afraid to use his intelligence to point out the blushing shame of human bestiality, that man, the beast, shuts his eyes to, trying to pretend it doesn't exist. And what about woman – what is she like? She looks at you invitingly, teasingly. You take her in your arms. But as soon as she feels your arms round her she closes her eyes. It's the sign of her mission, the sign by which she says to a man, 'Blind yourself – I'm blind!'

**Stepdaughter** And when she doesn't close her eyes any more? What then? When she doesn't feel the need to hide from herself any more, to shut her eyes and hide her own shame. When she can see instead, dispassionately and dry-eyed this blushing shame of a man who has blinded himself, who is without love. What then? Oh, then what disgust, what utter disgust she feels for all these intellectual complications, for all this philosophy that points to the bestiality of man and then tries to defend him, to excuse him . . . I can't listen to him, sir. Because when a man says he needs to 'simplify' life like this – reducing it to bestiality – and throws away every human scrap of innocent desire, genuine feeling, idealism, duty, modesty, shame, then there's nothing more contemptible and nauseating than his remorse – crocodile tears!

**Producer** Let's get to the point, let's get to the point. This is all chat.

**Father** Right then! But a fact is like a sack – it won't stand up if it's empty. To make it stand up, first you have to put in it all the reasons and feelings that caused it in the first place. I couldn't possibly have known that when that fellow died they'd come back here, that they were desperately poor and that the Mother had gone out to work as a dressmaker, nor that she'd gone to work for Madame Pace, of all people.

**Stepdaughter** She's a very high-class dressmaker – you must understand that. She apparently has only high-class customers, but she has arranged things carefully so that these high-class customers in fact serve her – they give her a respectable front . . . without spoiling things for the other ladies at the shop, who are not quite so high-class at all.

**Mother** Believe me, sir, the idea never entered my head that the old hag gave me work because she had an eye on my daughter . . .

**Stepdaughter** Poor Mummy! Do you know what that woman would do when I took back the work that my mother had been doing? She would point out how the dress had been ruined by giving it to my mother to sew: she bargained, she grumbled. So, you see, I paid for it, while this poor woman here thought she was sacrificing herself for me and these two children, sewing dresses all night for Madame Pace.

*The* **Actors** *make gestures and noises of disgust.*

**Producer** (*quickly*) And there one day, you met . . .

**Stepdaughter** (*pointing at the* **Father**) Yes, him. Oh, he was an old customer of hers! What a scene that's going to be, superb!

**Father** With her, the mother, arriving –

**Stepdaughter** (*quickly, viciously*) – Almost in time!

**Father** (*crying out*) – No, just in time, just in time! Because, luckily, I found out who she was in time. And I took them all back to my house, sir. Can you imagine the situation now, for the two of us living in the same house? She, just as you see her here: and I, not able to look her in the face.

**Stepdaughter** It's so absurd! Do you think it's possible for me, sir, after what happened at Madame Pace's, to pretend that I'm a modest little miss, well brought up and virtuous just so that I can fit in with his damned pretensions to a 'sound moral healthiness'?

**Father** This is the real drama for me; the belief that we all, you see, think of ourselves as one single person: but it's not true: each of us is several different people, and all these people live inside us. With one person we seem like this and with another we seem very different. But we always have the illusion of being the same person for everybody and of always being the same person in everything we do. But it's not true! It's not true! We find this out for ourselves very clearly when by some terrible chance we're suddenly stopped in the middle of doing something and we're left dangling there, suspended. We realise then, that every part of us was not involved in what we'd been doing and that it would be a dreadful injustice of other people to judge us only by this one action as we dangle there, hanging in chains, fixed for all eternity, as if the whole of one's personality were summed up in that single, interrupted action. Now do you understand this girl's treachery? She accidentally found me somewhere I shouldn't have been, doing something I shouldn't have been doing! She discovered a part of me that shouldn't have existed for her: and now she wants to fix on me a reality that I should never have had to assume for her: it came from a single brief and shameful moment in my life. This is what hurts me most of all. And you'll see that the play will make a tremendous impact from this idea of mine. But then, there's the position of the others. His . . . (*Pointing to the* **Son**.)

**Son** (*shrugging his shoulders scornfully*) Leave me out of it. I don't come into this.

**Father** Why don't you come into this?

**Son** I don't come into it and I don't want to come into it, because you know perfectly well that I wasn't intended to be mixed up with you lot.

**Stepdaughter** We're vulgar, common people, you see! He's a fine gentleman. But you've probably noticed that every now and then I look at him contemptuously, and when I do, he lowers his eyes – he knows the harm he's done me.

**Son** (*not looking at her*) I have?

**Stepdaughter** Yes, you. It's your fault, dearie, that I went on the streets! Your fault! (*Movement of horror from the* **Actors**.) Did you or didn't you, with your attitude, deny us – I won't say the intimacy of your home – but that simple hospitality that makes guests feel comfortable? We were intruders who had come to invade the country of your 'legitimacy'! (*Turning to the* **Producer**.) I'd like you to have seen some of the little scenes that went on between him and me, sir. He says that I tyrannised over everyone. But don't you see? It was because of the way he treated us. He called it 'vile' that I should insist on the right we had to move into his house with my mother – and she's his mother too. And I went into the house as its mistress.

**Son** (*slowly coming forward*) They're really enjoying themselves, aren't they, sir? It's easy when they all gang up against me. But try to imagine what happened: one fine day, there is a son sitting quietly at home and he sees arrive as bold as brass, a young woman like this, who cheekily asks for his father, and heaven knows what business she has with him. Then he sees her come back with the same brazen look in her eye accompanied by that little girl there: and he sees her treat his father – without knowing why – in a most ambiguous and insolent way – asking him for money in a tone that leads one to suppose he really ought to give it, because he is obliged to do so.

**Father** But I was obliged to do so: I owed it to your mother.

**Son** And how was I to know that? When had I ever seen her before? When had I ever heard her mentioned? Then one day I see her come in with her (*Pointing at the* **Stepdaughter**.), that boy and that little girl: they say to me, 'Oh, didn't you know? This is your mother, too.' Little by little I began to understand, mostly from her attitude

(*Points to* **Stepdaughter**.) why they'd come to live in the house so suddenly. I can't and I won't say what I feel, and what I think. I wouldn't even like to confess it to myself. So I can't take any active part in this. Believe me, sir, I am a character who has not been fully developed dramatically, and I feel uncomfortable, most uncomfortable, in their company. So please leave me out of it.

**Father** What! But it's precisely because you feel like this . . .

**Son** (*violently exasperated*) How do you know what I feel? When have you ever bothered yourself about me?

**Father** All right! I admit it! But isn't that a situation in itself? This withdrawing of yourself, it's cruel to me and to your mother: when she came back to the house, seeing you almost for the first time, not recognising you, but knowing that you're her own son . . . (*Turning to point out the* **Mother** *to the* **Producer**.) There, look at her: she's weeping.

**Stepdaughter** (*angrily, stamping her foot*) Like the fool she is!

**Father** (*quickly pointing at the* **Stepdaughter** *to the* **Producer**) She can't stand that young man, you know. (*Turning and referring to the* **Son**.) He says that he doesn't come into it, but he's really the pivot of the action! Look here at this little boy, who clings to his mother all the time, frightened, humiliated. And it's because of him over there! Perhaps this little boy's problem is the worst of all: he feels an outsider, more than the others do; he feels so mortified, so humiliated just being in the house – because it's charity, you see. (*Quietly*.) He's like his father: timid; he doesn't say anything . . .

**Producer** It's not a good idea at all, using him: you don't know what a nuisance children are on the stage.

**Father** He won't need to be on the stage for long. Nor will the little girl – she's the first to go.

**Producer** That's good! Yes. I tell you all this interests me – it interests me very much. I'm sure we've the material here for a good play.

**Stepdaughter** (*trying to push herself in*) With a character like me you have!

**Father** (*driving her off, wanting to hear what the* **Producer** *has decided*) You stay out of it!

**Producer** (*going on, ignoring the interruption*) It's new, yes.

**Father** Oh, it's absolutely new!

**Producer** You've got a nerve, though, haven't you, coming here and throwing it at me like this?

**Father** I'm sure you understand. Born as we are for the stage . . .

**Producer** Are you amateur actors?

**Father** No! I say we are born for the stage because . . .

**Producer** Come on now! You're an old hand at this, at acting!

**Father** No I'm not. I only act, as everyone does, the part in life that he's chosen for himself, or that others have chosen for him. And you can see that sometimes my own passion gets a bit out of hand, a bit theatrical, as it does with all of us.

**Producer** Maybe, maybe . . . But you do see, don't you, that without an author . . . I could give you someone's address . . .

**Father** Oh no! Look here! You do it.

**Producer** Me? What are you talking about?

**Father** Yes, you. Why not?

**Producer** Because I've never written anything!

**Father** Well, why not start now, if you don't mind my

suggesting it? There's nothing to it. Everybody's doing it. And your job is even easier, because we're here, all of us, alive before you.

**Producer** That's not enough.

**Father** Why isn't it enough? When you've seen us live our drama . . .

**Producer** Perhaps so. But we'll still need someone to write it.

**Father** Only to write it down, perhaps, while it happens in front of him – live – scene by scene. It'll be enough to sketch it out simply first and then run through it.

**Producer** (*coming back up, tempted by the idea*) Do you know I'm almost tempted . . . just for fun . . . it might work.

**Father** Of course it will. You'll see what wonderful scenes will come right out of it! I could tell you what they will be!

**Producer** You tempt me . . . you tempt me! We'll give it a chance. Come with me to the office. (*Turning to the* **Actors**.) Take a break: but don't go far away. Be back in a quarter of an hour or twenty minutes. (*To the* **Father**.) Let's see, let's try it out. Something extraordinary might come out of this.

**Father** Of course it will! Don't you think it'd be better if the others came too? (*Indicating the other* **Characters**.)

**Producer** Yes, come on, come on. (*Going, then turning to speak to the* **Actors**.) Don't forget: don't be late: back in a quarter of an hour.

*The* **Producer** *and the* **Six Characters** *cross the stage and go. The* **Actors** *look at each other in astonishment.*

**Leading Actor** Is he serious? What's he going to do?

**Young Actor** I think he's gone round the bend.

**Another Actor** Does he expect to make up a play in

five minutes?

**Young Actor** Yes, like the old actors in the *commedia dell'arte*!

**Leading Actress** Well if he thinks I'm going to appear in that sort of nonsense . . .

**Young Actor** Nor me!

**Fourth Actor** I should like to know who they are.

**Third Actor** Who do you think? They're probably escaped lunatics – or crooks.

**Young Actor** And is he taking them seriously?

**Young Actress** It's vanity. The vanity of seeing himself as an author.

**Leading Actor** I've never heard of such a thing! If the theatre, ladies and gentlemen, is reduced to this . . .

**Fifth Actor** I'm enjoying it!

**Third Actor** Really? We shall have to wait and see what happens next I suppose.

*Talking, they leave the stage. Some go out through the back door, some to the dressing-rooms.*

*The curtain stays up.*

*The interval lasts twenty minutes.*

# *Act Two*

*The theatre warning-bell sounds to call the audience back. From the dressing-rooms, the door at the back and even from the auditorium, the* **Actors**, *the* **Stage Manager**, *the* **Stage-hands**, *the* **Prompter**, *the* **Property Man** *and the* **Producer**, *accompanied by the* **Six Characters** *all come back on to the stage.*

*The house lights go out and the stage lights come on again.*

**Producer** Come on, everybody! Are we all here? Quiet now! Listen! Let's get started! Stage Manager?

**Stage Manager** Yes, I'm here.

**Producer** Give me that little parlour setting, will you? A couple of plain flats and a door flat will do. Hurry up with it!

*The* **Stage Manager** *runs off to order someone to do this immediately and at the same time the* **Producer** *is making arrangements with the* **Property Man**, the **Prompter**, *and the* **Actors***: the two flats and the door flat are painted in pink and gold stripes.*

**Producer** (*to* **Property Man**) Go see if we have a sofa in stock.

**Property Man** Yes, there's that green one.

**Stepdaughter** No, no, not a green one! It was yellow velvet with flowers on it: it was enormous! And so comfortable!

**Property Man** We haven't got one like that.

**Producer** It doesn't matter! Give me whatever there is.

**Stepdaughter** What do you mean, it doesn't matter? It was Madame Pace's famous sofa.

**Producer** It's only for a rehearsal! Please, don't interfere.

(*To the* **Stage Manager**.) Oh, and see if there's a shop window, will you – preferably a long, low one.

**Stepdaughter** And a little table, a little mahogany table for the blue envelope.

**Stage Manager** (*to the* **Producer**) There's that little gold one.

**Producer** That'll do – bring it.

**Father** A mirror!

**Stepdaughter** And a screen! A screen, please, or I won't be able to manage, will I?

**Stage Manager** All right. We've lots of big screens, don't you worry.

**Producer** (*to* **Stepdaughter**) Then don't you want some coat-hangers and some clothes racks?

**Stepdaughter** Yes, lots of them, lots of them.

**Producer** (*to the* **Stage Manager**) See how many there are and have them brought up.

**Stage Manager** Right, I'll see to it.

*The* **Stage Manager** *goes off to do it: and while the* **Producer** *is talking to the* **Prompter**, *the* **Characters** *and the* **Actors**, *the* **Stage Manager** *is telling the* **Scene Shifters** *where to set up the furniture they have brought.*

**Producer** (*to the* **Prompter**) Now you, go sit down, will you? Look, this is an outline of the play, act by act. (*He hands him several sheets of paper.*) But you'll need to be on your toes.

**Prompter** Shorthand?

**Producer** (*pleasantly surprised*) Oh, good! You know shorthand?

**Prompter** I don't know much about prompting, but I do know about shorthand.

**Producer** Thank God for that anyway! (*He turns to a* **Stage-hand**.) Go fetch me some paper from my office – lots of it – as much as you can find!

*The* **Stage-hand** *goes running off and then comes back shortly with a bundle of paper that he gives to the* **Prompter**.

**Producer** (*crossing to the* **Prompter**) Follow the scenes, one after another, as they are played and try to get the lines down . . . at least the most important ones. (*Then turning to the* **Actors**.) Get out of the way everybody! Here, go over to the prompt side (*Pointing to stage left.*) and pay attention!

**Leading Actress** But, excuse me, we . . .

**Producer** (*anticipating her*) You won't be expected to improvise, don't worry!

**Leading Actor** Then what are we expected to do?

**Producer** Nothing! Just go over there, listen and watch. You'll all be given your parts later written out. Right now we're going to rehearse, as well as we can. And they will be doing the rehearsal. (*He points to the* **Characters**.)

**Father** (*rather bewildered, as if he had fallen from the clouds into the middle of the confusion on the stage*) We are? Excuse me, but what do you mean, a rehearsal?

**Producer** I mean a rehearsal – a rehearsal for the benefit of the actors. (*Pointing to the* **Actors**.)

**Father** But if we are the characters . . .

**Producer** That's right, you're 'the characters': but characters don't act here, my dear chap. It's actors who act here. The characters are there in the script – (*Pointing to the* **Prompter**.) that's when there is a script.

**Father** That's the point! Since there isn't one and you have the luck to have the characters alive in front of you . . .

**Producer** Great! You want to do everything yourselves, do you? To act your own play, to produce your own play!

**Father** Well yes, just as we are.

**Producer** That would be an experience for us, I can tell you!

**Leading Actor** And what about us? What would we be doing then?

**Producer** Don't tell me you think you know how to act! Don't make me laugh! (*The* **Actors** *in fact laugh.*) There you are, you see, you've made them laugh. (*Then remembering.*) But let's get back to the point! We need to cast the play. Well, that's easy: it almost casts itself. (*To the* **Second Actress**.) You, the Mother. (*To the* **Father**.) You'll need to give her a name.

**Father** Amalia.

**Producer** But that's the real name of your wife isn't it? We can't use her real name.

**Father** But why not? That is her name . . . But perhaps if this lady is to play the part . . . (*Indicating the* **Actress** *vaguely with a wave of his hand.*) I think of her as Amalia . . . (*Pointing to the* **Mother**.) But do as you like . . . (*A little confused.*) I don't know what to say . . . I'm already starting to . . . how can I explain it . . . to sound false, my own words sound like someone else's.

**Producer** Now don't worry yourself about it, don't worry about it at all. We'll work out the right tone of voice. As for the name, if you want it to be Amalia, then Amalia it shall be: or we can find another. For the moment we'll refer to the characters like this: (*To the* **Young Actor**, *the juvenile lead.*) you are the Son. (*To the* **Leading Actress**.) You, of course, are the Stepdaughter.

**Stepdaughter** (*excitedly*) What did you say? That woman is me? (*Bursts into laughter.*)

**Producer** (*angrily*) What are you laughing at?

**Leading Actress** (*indignantly*) Nobody has ever dared to laugh at me before! Either you treat me with respect or I'm walking out! (*Starting to go.*)

**Stepdaughter** I'm sorry. I wasn't really laughing at you.

**Producer** (*to the* **Stepdaughter**) You should feel proud to be played by . . .

**Leading Actress** (*quickly, scornfully*) . . . that woman!

**Stepdaughter** But I wasn't thinking about her, honestly. I was thinking about me: I can't see myself in you at all . . . you're not a bit like me!

**Father** Yes, that's right: you see, our meaning . . .

**Producer** What are you talking about, 'our meaning'? Do you think you have exclusive rights to what you represent? Do you think it can only exist inside you? Not a bit of it!

**Father** What? Don't we even have our own meaning?

**Producer** Not a bit of it! Whatever you mean is only material here, to which the actors give form and body, voice and gesture, and who, through their art, have given expression to much better material than what you have to offer: yours is really very trivial and if it stands up on the stage, the credit, believe me, will all be due to my actors.

**Father** I don't dare to contradict you. But you for your part, must believe me – it doesn't seem trivial to us. We are suffering terribly now, with these bodies, these faces . . .

**Producer** (*interrupting impatiently*) Yes, well, the make-up will change that, make-up will change that, at least as far as the faces are concerned.

**Father** Yes, but the voices, the gestures . . .

**Producer** That's enough! You can't come on the stage here as yourselves. It is our actors who will represent you here: and let that be the end of it!

**Father** I understand that. But now I think I see why our author who saw us alive as we are here now, didn't want to put us on the stage. I don't want to offend your actors. God forbid that I should! But I think that if I saw myself represented . . . by I don't know whom . . .

**Leading Actor** (*rising majestically and coming forward, followed by a laughing group of* **Young Actresses**) By me, if you don't object.

**Father** (*respectfully, smoothly*) I shall be honoured, sir. (*He bows.*) But I think that no matter how hard this gentleman works with all his will and all his art to identify himself with me . . . (*He stops, confused.*)

**Leading Actor** Yes, go on.

**Father** Well, I was saying the performance he will give, even if he is made up to look like me . . . I mean with the difference in our appearance . . . (*All the* **Actors** *laugh.*) it will be difficult for it to be a performance of me as I really am. It will be more like – well, not just because of his figure – it will be more an interpretation of what I am, what he believes me to be, and not how I know myself to be. And it seems to me that this should be taken into account by those who are going to comment on us.

**Producer** So you are already worrying about what the critics will say, are you? And I'm still waiting to get this thing started! The critics can say what they like: and we'll worry about putting on the play. If we can! (*Stepping out of the group and looking around.*) Come on, come on! Is the scene set for us yet? (*To the* **Actors** *and* **Characters**.) Out of the way! Let's have a look at it. (*Climbing down off the stage.*) Don't let's waste any more time. (*To the* **Stepdaughter**.) Does it look all right to you?

**Stepdaughter** What? That? I don't recognise it at all.

**Producer** Good God! Did you expect us to reconstruct

the room at the back of Madame Pace's shop here on the stage? (*To the* **Father**.) Did you say the room had flowered wallpaper?

**Father** White, yes.

**Producer** Well it's not white: it's striped. That sort of thing doesn't matter at all! As for the furniture, it looks to me as if we have nearly everything we need. Move that little table a bit further downstage. (*A* **Stage-hand** *does it. To the* **Property Man**.) Go and fetch an envelope, pale blue if you can find one, and give it to that gentleman there. (*Pointing to the* **Father**.)

**Stage-hand** An envelope for letters?

**Producer**
**Father** } Yes, an envelope for letters!

**Stage-hand** Right. (*He goes off.*)

**Producer** Now then, come on! The first scene is the young lady's. (*The* **Leading Actress** *comes to the centre.*) No, no, not yet. I said the young lady's. (*He points to the* **Stepdaughter**.) You stay there and watch.

**Stepdaughter** (*adding quickly*) . . . how I bring it to life.

**Leading Actress** (*resenting this*) I shall know how to bring it to life, don't worry, when I am allowed to.

**Producer** (*his head in his hands*) Ladies, please, no more arguments! Now then. The first scene is between the young lady and Madame Pace. Oh! (*Worried, turning round and looking out into the auditorium.*) Where is Madame Pace?

**Father** She isn't here with us.

**Producer** So what do we do now?

**Father** But she is real. She's real too!

**Producer** All right. So where is she?

**Father** May I deal with this? (*Turns to the* **Actresses**.) Would each of you ladies be kind enough to lend me a hat, a coat, a scarf or something?

**Actresses** (*some are surprised or amused*) What? My scarf? A coat? What's he want my hat for? What are you wanting to do with them? (*All the* **Actresses** *are laughing.*)

**Father** Oh, nothing much, just hang them up here on the racks for a minute or two. Perhaps someone would be kind enough to lend me a coat?

**Actors** Just a coat? Come on, more! The man must be mad.

**An Actress** What for? Only my coat?

**Father** Yes, to hang up here, just for a moment. I'm very grateful to you. Do you mind?

**Actresses** (*taking off various hats, coats, scarves, laughing and going to hang them on the racks*) Why not? Here you are. I really think it's crazy. Is it to dress the set?

**Father** Yes, exactly. It's to dress the set.

**Producer** Would you mind telling me what you are doing?

**Father** Yes, of course: perhaps, if we dress the set better, she will be drawn by the articles of her trade and, who knows, she may even come to join us . . . (*He invites them to watch the door at the back of the set.*) Look! Look!

*The door at the back opens and* **Madame Pace** *takes a few steps downstage: she is a gross old harridan wearing a ludicrous carroty-coloured wig with a single red rose stuck in at one side, Spanish fashion, garishly made-up, in a vulgar but stylish red silk dress, holding an ostrich-feather fan in one hand and a cigarette between two fingers in the other. At the sight of this apparition, the* **Actors** *and the* **Producer** *immediately jump off the stage with cries of fear, leaping down into the auditorium and up the aisles. The* **Stepdaughter**, *however, runs across to* **Madame Pace**, *and* *greets her respectfully, as if she were the mistress.*

**Stepdaughter** (*running across to her*) Here she is! Here she is!

**Father** (*smiling broadly*) It's her! What did I tell you? Here she is!

**Producer** (*recovering from his shock, indignantly*) What sort of trick is this?

**Leading Actor** (*almost at the same time as the others*) What the hell is happening?

**Juvenile Lead** Where on earth did they get that extra from?

**Young Actress** They were keeping her hidden!

**Leading Actress** It's a game, a conjuring trick!

**Father** Wait a minute! Why do you want to spoil a miracle by being factual. Can't you see this is a miracle of reality, that is born, brought to life, lured here, reproduced, just for the sake of this scene, with more right to be alive here than you have? Perhaps it has more truth than you have yourselves. Which actress can improve on Madame Pace there? Well? That is the real Madame Pace. You must admit that the actress who plays her will be less true than she is herself – and there she is in person! Look! My daughter recognised her straight away and went to meet her. Now watch – just watch this scene.

*Hesitantly, the* **Producer** *and the* **Actors** *move back to their original places on the stage.*

*But the scene between the* **Stepdaughter** *and* **Madame Pace** *has already begun while the* **Actors** *were protesting and the* **Father** *explaining: it is being played under their breaths, very quietly, very naturally, in a way that is obviously impossible on stage. So when the* **Actors***' attention is recalled by the* **Father** *they turn and see that* **Madame Pace** *has just put her hand under the* **Stepdaughter***'s chin to make her lift her head up; they also hear* *her speak in a way that is unintelligible to them. They watch and listen hard for a few moments, then they start to make fun of them.*

**Producer** Well?

**Leading Actor** What's she saying?

**Leading Actress** Can't hear a thing!

**Juvenile Lead** Louder! Speak up!

**Stepdaughter** (*leaving* **Madame Pace** *who has an astonishing smile on her face, and coming down to the* **Actors**) Louder? What do you mean, 'Louder'? What we're talking about you can't talk about loudly. I could shout about it a moment ago to embarrass him (*Pointing to the* **Father**.) to shame him and to get my own back on him! But it's a different matter for Madame Pace. It would mean prison for her.

**Producer** What the hell are you on about? Here in the theatre you have to make yourself heard! Don't you see that? We can't hear you even from here, and we're on the stage with you! Imagine what it would be like with an audience out front! You need to make the scene go! And after all, you would speak normally to each other when you're alone, and you will be, because we shan't be here anyway. I mean we're only here because it's a rehearsal. So just imagine that there you are in the room at the back of the shop, and there's no one to hear you.

*The* **Stepdaughter**, *with a knowing smile, wags her finger and her head rather elegantly, as if to say no.*

**Producer** Why not?

**Stepdaughter** (*mysteriously, whispering loudly*) Because there is someone who will hear if she speaks normally. (*Pointing to* **Madame Pace**.)

**Producer** (*anxiously*) You're not going to make someone else appear are you?

*The* **Actors** *get ready to dive off the stage again.*

**Father** No, no. She means me. I ought to be over there, waiting behind the door: and Madame Pace knows I'm there, so excuse me will you: I'll go there now so that I shall be ready for my entrance.

*He goes towards the back of the stage.*

**Producer** (*stopping him*) No, no wait a minute! You must remember the stage conventions! Before you can go on to that part . . .

**Stepdaughter** (*interrupts him*) Oh yes, let's get on with that part. Now! Now! I'm dying to do that scene. If he wants to go through it now, I'm ready!

**Producer** (*shouting*) But before that we must have, clearly stated, the scene between you and her. (*Pointing to* **Madame Pace**.) Do you see?

**Stepdaughter** Oh God! She's only told me what you already know, that my mother's needlework is badly done again, the dress is spoilt and that I shall have to be patient if I want her to go on helping us out of our mess.

**Madame Pace** (*coming forward, with a great air of importance*) Ah, yes, sir, for that I do not wish to make a profit, to make advantage.

**Producer** (*half frightened*) What? Does she really speak like that?

*All the* **Actors** *burst out laughing.*

**Stepdaughter** (*laughing too*) Yes, she speaks like that, half in Spanish, in the silliest way imaginable!

**Madame Pace** Ah it is not good manners that you laugh at me when I make myself to speak, as I can, English, senor.

**Producer** No, no, you're right! Speak like that, please speak like that, madam. It'll be marvellous. Couldn't be better! It'll add a little touch of comedy to a rather crude situation. Speak like that! It'll be great!

**Stepdaughter** Great! Why not? When you hear a proposition made in that sort of accent, it'll almost seem like a joke, won't it? Perhaps you'll want to laugh when you hear that there's an 'old senor' who wants to 'amuse himself with me' – isn't that right, Madame?

**Madame Pace** Not so old . . . but not quite young, no? But if he is not to your taste . . . he is, how you say, discreet!

*The* **Mother** *leaps up, to the astonishment and dismay of the* **Actors** *who had not been paying any attention to her, so that when she shouts out they are startled and then smilingly restrain her: however she has already snatched off* **Madame Pace***'s wig and flung it on the floor.*

**Mother** You witch! Witch! Murderess! Oh, my daughter!

**Stepdaughter** (*running across and taking hold of the* **Mother**) No! No! Mother! Please!

**Father** (*running across to her as well*) Calm yourself, calm yourself! Come and sit down.

**Mother** Get her away from here!

**Stepdaughter** (*to the* **Producer** *who has also crossed to her*) My mother can't bear to be in the same place with her.

**Father** (*also speaking quietly to the* **Producer**) They can't possibly be in the same place! That's why she wasn't with us when we first came, do you see! If they meet, everything's given away from the very beginning.

**Producer** It's not important, that's not important! This is only a first run-through at the moment! It's all useful stuff, even if it is confused. I'll sort it all out later. (*Turning to the* **Mother** *and taking her to sit down on her chair.*) Come on my dear, take it easy, take it easy: come and sit down again.

**Stepdaughter** Go on, Madame Pace.

**Madame Pace** (*offended*) Oh no, thank you! I no longer do nothing here with your mother present.

**Stepdaughter** Get on with it, bring in this 'old senor' who wants to 'amuse himself with me'! (*Turning majestically to the others.*) You see, this next scene has got to be played out – we must do it now. (*To* **Madame Pace**.) Oh, you can go!

**Madame Pace** Ah, I go, I go – I go! Most probably I go!

*She leaves banging her wig back into place, glaring furiously at the* **Actors** *who applaud her exit, laughing loudly.*

**Stepdaughter** (*to the* **Father**) Now you come on! No, you don't need to go off again! Come back! Pretend you've just come in! Look, I'm standing here with my eyes on the ground, modestly – well, come on, speak up! Use that special sort of voice, like somebody who has just come in. 'Good afternoon, my dear.'

**Producer** (*off the stage by now*) Look here, who's the director here, you or me? (*To the* **Father** *who looks uncertain and bewildered.*) Go on, do as she says: go upstage – no, no don't bother to make an entrance. Then come downstage again.

*The* **Father** *does as he is told, half mesmerised. He is very pale but already involved in the reality of his recreated life, smiles as he draws near the back of the stage, almost as if he genuinely is not aware of the drama that is about to sweep over him. The* **Actors** *are immediately intent on the scene that is beginning now.*

**The Scene**

**Father** (*coming forward with a new note in his voice*) Good afternoon, my dear.

**Stepdaughter** (*her head down trying to hide her fright*) Good afternoon.

**Father** (*studying her a little under the brim of her hat which partly hides her face from him and seeing that she is very young, exclaims to* *himself a little complacently and a little guardedly because of the danger of being compromised in a risky adventure)* Ah . . . but . . . tell me, this won't be the first time, will it? The first time you've been here?

**Stepdaughter** No, sir.

**Father** You've been here before? (*And after the* **Stepdaughter** *has nodded an answer.*) More than once? (*He waits for her reply, tries again to look at her under the brim of her hat, smiles, then says.*) Well then . . . it shouldn't be too . . . May I take off your hat?

**Stepdaughter** (*quickly, to stop him, unable to conceal her shudder of fear and disgust*) No, don't! I'll do it!

*She takes it off unsteadily.*

*The* **Mother** *watches the scene intently with the* **Son** *and the two smaller children who cling close to her all the time: they make a group on one side of the stage opposite the* **Actors**. *She follows the words and actions of the* **Father** *and the* **Stepdaughter** *in this scene with a variety of expressions on her face – sadness, dismay, anxiety, horror; sometimes she turns her face away and sobs.*

**Mother** Oh God! Oh God!

**Father** (*he stops as if turned to stone by the sobbing; then he goes on in the same tone of voice*) Here, give it to me. I'll hang it up for you. (*He takes the hat in his hand.*) But such a pretty, dear little head like yours should have a much smarter hat than this! Would you like to help me choose one, then, from these hats of Madame's hanging up here? Would you?

**Young Actress** (*interrupting*) Be careful! Those are our hats!

**Producer** (*quickly and angrily*) For God's sake, shut up! Don't try to be funny! We're rehearsing! (*Turns back to the* **Stepdaughter**.) Please go on, will you, from where you were interrupted.

**Stepdaughter** (*going on*) No, thank you, sir.

**Father** Oh, don't say no to me please! Say you'll have one – to please me. Isn't this a pretty one – look! And then it will please Madame too, you know. She's put them out here on purpose, of course.

**Stepdaughter** No, look, I could never wear it.

**Father** Are you thinking of what they would say at home when you went in wearing a new hat? Goodness me! Don't you know what to do? Shall I tell you what to say at home?

**Stepdaughter** (*furiously, nearly exploding*) That's not why! I couldn't wear it because . . . as you can see: you should have noticed it before. (*Indicating her black dress.*)

**Father** You're in mourning! Oh, forgive me. You're right, I see that now. Please forgive me. Believe me, I'm really very sorry.

**Stepdaughter** (*gathering all her strength and making herself overcome her contempt and revulsion*) That's enough. Don't go on, that's enough. I ought to be thanking you and not letting you blame yourself and get upset. Don't think any more about what I told you, please. And I should do the same. (*Forcing herself to smile and adding.*) I should try to forget that I'm dressed like this.

**Producer** (*interrupting, turning to the* **Prompter** *in the box and jumping up on the stage again*) Hold it, hold it! Don't put that last line down, leave it out. (*Turning to the* **Father** *and the* **Stepdaughter**.) It's going well! It's going well! (*Then to the* **Father** *alone.*) Then we'll put in there the bit that we talked about. (*To the* **Actors**.) That scene with the hats is good, isn't it?

**Stepdaughter** But the best bit is coming now! Why can't we get on with it?

**Producer** Just be patient, wait a minute. (*Turning and moving across to the* **Actors**.) Of course, it'll all have to be made a lot more light-hearted.

**Leading Actor** We shall have to play it a lot quicker, I think.

**Leading Actress** Of course: there's nothing particularly difficult in it. (*To the* **Leading Actor**.) Shall we run through it now?

**Leading Actor** Yes right . . . Shall we take it from my entrance? (*He goes to his position behind the door upstage.*)

**Producer** (*to the* **Leading Actress**) Now then, listen, imagine the scene between you and Madame Pace is finished. I'll write it up myself properly later on. You ought to be over here I think – (*She goes the opposite way.*) Where are you going now?

**Leading Actress** Just a minute, I want to get my hat – (*She crosses to take her hat from the stand.*)

**Producer** Right, good, ready now? You are standing here with your head down.

**Stepdaughter** (*very amused*) But she's not dressed in black!

**Leading Actress** Oh, but I shall be, and I'll look a lot better than you do, darling.

**Producer** (*to the* **Stepdaughter**) Shut up, will you! Go over there and watch! You might learn something! (*Clapping his hands.*) Right! Come on! Quiet please! Take it from his entrance.

*He climbs off stage so that he can see better. The door opens at the back of the set and the* **Leading Actor** *enters with the lively, knowing air of an ageing roué. The playing of the following scene by the* **Actors** *must seem from the very beginning to be something quite different from the earlier scene, but without having the faintest air of parody in it.*

*Naturally the* **Stepdaughter** *and the* **Father**, *unable to see themselves in the* **Leading Actor** *and* **Leading Actress**, *hearing their words said by them, express their reactions in different ways, by gestures, or smiles or obvious protests so that we are aware* *of their suffering, their astonishment, their disbelief.*

*The* **Prompter***'s voice is heard clearly between every line in the scene, telling the* **Actors** *what to say next.*

**Leading Actor** Good afternoon, my dear.

**Father** (*immediately, unable to restrain himself*) Oh, no!

*The* **Stepdaughter**, *watching the* **Leading Actor** *enter this way, bursts into laughter.*

**Producer** (*furious*) Shut up, for God's sake! And don't you dare laugh like that! We're never going to get anywhere at this rate.

**Stepdaughter** (*coming to the front*) I'm sorry, I can't help it! The lady stands exactly where you told her to stand and she never moved. But if it were me and I heard someone say good afternoon to me in that way and with a voice like that I should burst out laughing – so I did.

**Father** (*coming down a little too*) Yes, she's right, the whole manner, the voice . . .

**Producer** To hell with the manner and the voice! Get out of the way, will you, and let me watch the rehearsal!

**Leading Actor** (*coming downstage*) If I have to play an old man who has come to a knocking shop –

**Producer** Take no notice, ignore them. Go on please! It's going well, it's going well! (*He waits for the* **Actors** *to begin again.*) Right, again!

**Leading Actor** Good afternoon, my dear.

**Leading Actress** Good afternoon.

**Leading Actor** (*copying the gestures of the* **Father**, *looking under the brim of the hat, but expressing distinctly the two emotions, first, complacent satisfaction and then anxiety*) Ah! But tell me . . . this won't be the first time I hope.

**Father** (*instinctively correcting him*) Not 'I hope' – 'will it', 'will it'.

**Producer** Say 'will it' – and it's a question.

**Leading Actor** (*glaring at the* **Prompter**) I distinctly heard him say 'I hope'.

**Producer** So what? It's all the same, 'I hope' or 'isn't it'. It doesn't make any difference. Carry on, carry on. But perhaps it should still be a little bit lighter; I'll show you – watch me! (*He climbs up on the stage again, and going back to the entrance, he does it himself.*) Good afternoon, my dear.

**Leading Actress** Good afternoon.

**Producer** Ah, tell me . . . (*He turns to the* **Leading Actor** *to make sure that he has seen the way he has demonstrated of looking under the brim of the hat.*) You see – surprise . . . anxiety and self-satisfaction. (*Then, starting again, he turns to the* **Leading Actress**.) This won't be the first time, will it? The first time you've been here? (*Again turns to the* **Leading Actor**, *questioningly.*) Right? (*To the* **Leading Actress**.) And then she says, 'No, sir'. (*Again to* **Leading Actor**.) See what I mean? More subtlety. (*And he climbs off the stage.*)

**Leading Actress** No, sir.

**Leading Actor** You've been here before? More than once?

**Producer** No, no, no! Wait for it, wait for it. Let her answer first. 'You've been here before?'

*The* **Leading Actress** *lifts her head a little, her eyes closed in pain and disgust, and when the* **Producer** *says 'Now' she nods her head twice.*

**Stepdaughter** (*involuntarily*) Oh, my God! (*And she immediately claps her hand over her mouth to stifle her laughter.*)

**Producer** What now?

**Stepdaughter** (*quickly*) Nothing, nothing!

**Producer** (*to* **Leading Actor**) Come on, then, now it's you.

**Leading Actor** More than once? Well then, it shouldn't be too . . . May I take off your hat?

*The* **Leading Actor** *says this last line in such a way and adds to it such a gesture that the* **Stepdaughter**, *even with her hand over her mouth trying to stop herself laughing, can't prevent a noisy burst of laughter.*

**Leading Actress** (*indignantly turning*) I'm not staying any longer to be laughed at by that woman!

**Leading Actor** Nor am I! That's the end – no more!

**Producer** (*to* **Stepdaughter**, *shouting*) Once and for all, will you shut up! Shut up!

**Stepdaughter** Yes, I'm sorry . . . I'm sorry.

**Producer** You're an ill-mannered little bitch! That's what you are! And you've gone too far this time!

**Father** (*trying to interrupt*) Yes, you're right, she went too far, but please forgive her . . .

**Producer** (*jumping on the stage*) Why should I forgive her? Her behaviour is intolerable!

**Father** Yes, it is, but the scene made such a peculiar impact on us . . .

**Producer** Peculiar? What do you mean peculiar? Why peculiar?

**Father** I'm full of admiration for your actors, for this gentleman (*To the* **Leading Actor**.) and this lady (*To the* **Leading Actress**.). But, you see, well . . . they're not us!

**Producer** Right! They're not! They're actors!

**Father** That's just the point – they're actors. And they are acting our parts very well, both of them. But that's what's different. However much they want to be the same as us, they're not.

**Producer** But why aren't they? What is it now?

**Father** It's something to do with . . . being themselves, I suppose, not being us.

**Producer** Well we can't do anything about that! I've told you already. You can't play the parts yourselves.

**Father** Yes, I know, I know . . .

**Producer** Right then. That's enough of that. (*Turning back to the* **Actors**.) We'll rehearse this later on our own, as we usually do. It's always a bad idea to have rehearsals with authors there! They're never satisfied. (*Turns back to the* **Father** *and the* **Stepdaughter**.) Come on, let's get on with it; and let's see if it's possible to do it without laughing.

**Stepdaughter** I won't laugh any more, I won't really. My best bit's coming up now, you wait and see!

**Producer** Right: when you say 'Don't think any more about what I told you, please. And I should do the same.' (*Turning to the* **Father**.) Then you come in immediately with the line 'I understand, ah yes, I understand' and then you ask . . .

**Stepdaughter** (*interrupting*) Ask what? What does he ask?

**Producer** Why you're in mourning.

**Stepdaughter** No! No! That's not right! Look: when I said that I should try not to think about the way I was dressed, do you know what he said? 'Well then, let's take it off, we'll take it off at once, shall we, your little black dress.'

**Producer** That's great! That'll be wonderful! That'll bring the house down!

**Stepdaughter** But it's the truth!

**Producer** The truth! Do me a favour will you? This is the theatre you know! Truth's all very well up to a point but . . .

**Stepdaughter** What do you want to do then?

**Producer** You'll see! You'll see! Leave it all to me.

**Stepdaughter** No. No I won't. I know what you want to do! Out of my feeling of revulsion, out of all the vile and sordid reasons why I am what I am, you want to make a sugary little sentimental romance. You want him to ask me why I'm in mourning and you want me to reply with the tears running down my face that it is only two months since my father died. No. No. I won't have it! He must say to me what he really did say. 'Well then, let's take it off, we'll take it off at once, shall we, your little black dress.' And I, with my heart still grieving for my father's death only two months before, I went behind there, do you see? Behind that screen and with my fingers trembling with shame and loathing I took off the dress, unfastened my bra . . .

**Producer** (*his head in his hands*) For God's sake! What are you saying!

**Stepdaughter** (*shouting excitedly*) The truth! I'm telling you the truth!

**Producer** All right then. Now listen to me. I'm not denying it's the truth. Right. And believe me I understand your horror, but you must see that we can't really put a scene like that on the stage.

**Stepdaughter** You can't? Then thanks very much. I'm not stopping here.

**Producer** No, listen . . .

**Stepdaughter** No, I'm going. I'm not stopping. The pair of you have worked it all out together, haven't you, what to put in the scene. Well, thank you very much! I understand everything now! He wants to get to the scene where he can talk about his spiritual torments but I want to show you my drama! Mine!

**Producer** (*shaking with anger*) Now we're getting to the real truth of it, aren't we? Your drama – yours! But it's not only yours, you know. It's drama for the other people as well! For him (*Pointing to the* **Father**.) and for your mother! You can't have one character coming on like you're doing, trampling over the others, taking over the play. Everything needs to be balanced and in harmony so that we can show what has to be shown! I know perfectly well that we've all got a life inside us and that we all want to parade it in front of other people. But that's the difficulty, how to present only the bits that are necessary in relation to the other characters, and in the small amount we show, to hint at all the rest of the inner life of the character! I agree, it would be so much simpler, if each character, in a soliloquy or in a lecture could pour out to the audience what's bubbling away inside him. But that's not the way we work. (*In an indulgent, placating tone.*) You must restrain yourself, you see. And believe me, it's in your own interests: because you could so easily make a bad impression, with all this uncontrollable anger, this disgust and exasperation. That seems a bit odd, if you don't mind my saying so, when you've admitted that you'd been with other men at Madame Pace's and more than once.

**Stepdaughter** I suppose that's true. But you know, all the other men were all him as far as I was concerned.

**Producer** (*not understanding*) Uum – ? What? What are you talking about?

**Stepdaughter** If someone falls into evil ways, isn't the responsibility for all the evil which follows to be laid at the door of the person who caused the first mistake? And in my case, it's him, from before I was even born. Look at him: see if it isn't true.

**Producer** Right then! What about the weight of remorse he's carrying? Isn't that important? Then, give him the chance to show it to us.

**Stepdaughter** But how? How on earth can he show all his long-suffering remorse, all his moral torments as he calls them, if you don't let him show his horror when he finds me in his arms one fine day, after he had asked me to take my dress off, a black dress for my father who had just died, and he finds that I'm the child he used to go and watch as she came out of school, me, a woman now, and a woman he could buy. (*She says these last words in a voice trembling with emotion.*)

*The* **Mother**, *hearing her say this, is overcome and at first gives way to stifled sobs, but then she bursts out into uncontrollable crying. Everyone is deeply moved. There is a long pause.*

**Stepdaughter** (*as soon as the* **Mother** *has quietened herself, goes on, firmly and thoughtfully*) At the moment we are here on our own and the public doesn't know about us. But tomorrow you will present us and our story in whatever way you choose, I suppose. But wouldn't you like to see the real drama? Wouldn't you like to see it explode into life, as it really did?

**Producer** Of course, nothing I'd like better, then I can use as much of it as possible.

**Stepdaughter** Then persuade my mother to leave.

**Mother** (*rising and her quiet weeping changing to a loud cry*) No! No! Don't let her! Don't let her do it!

**Producer** But they're only doing it for me to watch – only for me, do you see?

**Mother** I can't bear it, I can't bear it!

**Producer** But if it's already happened, I can't see what's the objection.

**Mother** No! It's happening now, as well: it's happening all the time. I'm not acting my suffering! Can't you understand that? I'm alive and here now but I can never forget that terrible moment of agony, that repeats itself endlessly and vividly in my mind. And these two little children here, you've never heard them speak have you? That's because they don't speak any more, not now. They just cling to me all the time: they help to keep my grief alive, but they don't really exist for themselves any more, not for themselves. And she (*Indicating the* **Stepdaughter**.) . . . she has gone away, left me completely, she's lost to me, lost . . . you see her here for one reason only: to keep perpetually before me, always real, the anguish and the torment I've suffered on her account.

**Father** The eternal moment, as I told you, sir. She is here (*Indicating the* **Stepdaughter**.) to keep me too in that moment, trapped for all eternity, chained and suspended in that one fleeting shameful moment of my life. She can't give up her role and you cannot rescue me from it.

**Producer** But I'm not saying that we won't present that bit. Not at all! It will be the climax of the first act, when she (*He points to the* **Mother**.) surprises you.

**Father** That's right, because that is the moment when I am sentenced: all our suffering should reach a climax in her cry. (*Again indicating the* **Mother**.)

**Stepdaughter** I can still hear it ringing in my ears! It was that cry that sent me mad! You can have me played just as you like: it doesn't matter! Dressed, too, if you want, so long as I can have at least an arm – only an arm – bare, because, you see, as I was standing like this (*She moves across to the* **Father** *and leans her head on his chest.*) with my head like this and my arms round his neck, I saw a vein, here in my arm, throbbing: and then it was almost as if that throbbing vein filled me with a shivering fear, and I shut my eyes tightly like this, like this and buried my head in his chest. (*Turning to the* **Mother**.) Scream, Mummy, scream. (*She buries her head in the* **Father***'s chest, and with her shoulders raised as if to try not to hear the scream, she speaks with a voice tense with suffering.*) Scream, as you screamed then!

**Mother** (*coming forward to pull them apart*) No! She's my daughter! My daughter! (*Tearing her from him.*) You brute, you animal, she's my daughter! Can't you see she's my daughter?

**Producer** (*retreating as far as the footlights while the* **Actors** *are full of dismay*) Marvellous! Yes, that's great! And then curtain, curtain!

**Father** (*running downstage to him, excitedly*) That's it, that's it! Because it really was like that!

**Producer** (*full of admiration and enthusiasm*) Yes, yes, that's got to be the curtain line! Curtain! Curtain!

*At the repeated calls of the* **Producer**, *the* **Stage Manager** *lowers the curtain, leaving on the apron in front, the* **Producer** *and the* **Father**.

**Producer** (*looking up to heaven with his arms raised*) The idiots! I didn't mean now! The bloody idiots – dropping it in on us like that! (*To the* **Father**, *and lifting up a corner of the curtain.*) That's marvellous! Really marvellous! A terrific effect! We'll end the act like that! It's the best tag line I've heard for ages. What a first act ending! I couldn't have done better if I'd written it myself!

*They go through the curtain together.*

# Act Three

*When the curtain goes up we see that the* **Stage Manager** *and* **Stage-hands** *have struck the first scene and have set another, a small garden fountain.*

*From one side of the stage the* **Actors** *come on and from the other the* **Characters**. *The* **Producer** *is standing in the middle of the stage with his hand over his mouth, thinking.*

**Producer** (*after a short pause, shrugging his shoulders*) Well, then: let's get on to the second act! Leave it all to me, and everything will work out properly.

**Stepdaughter** This is where we go to live at his house (*Pointing to the* **Father**.) in spite of the objections of him over there. (*Pointing to the* **Son**.)

**Producer** (*getting impatient*) All right, all right! But leave it all to me, will you?

**Stepdaughter** Provided that you make it clear that he objected!

**Mother** (*from the corner, shaking her head*) That doesn't matter! The worse it was for us, the more he suffered from remorse.

**Producer** (*impatiently*) I know, I know! I'll take it all into account. Don't worry!

**Mother** (*pleading*) To set my mind at rest, sir, please do make sure it's clear that I tried all I could –

**Stepdaughter** (*interrupting her scornfully and going on*) – to pacify me, to persuade me that this despicable creature wasn't worth making trouble about! (*To the* **Producer**.) Go on, set her mind at rest, because it's true, she tried very hard. I'm having a whale of a time now! You can see, can't you, that the meeker she was and the more she tried to worm her way into his heart, the more lofty and distant he became! How's that for a dramatic situation!

**Producer** Do you think that we can actually begin the second act?

**Stepdaughter** I won't say another word! But you'll see that it won't be possible to play everything in the garden, like you want to do.

**Producer** Why not?

**Stepdaughter** (*pointing to the* **Son**) Because to start with, he stays shut up in his room in the house all the time! And then all the scenes for this poor little devil of a boy happen in the house. I've told you once.

**Producer** Yes, I know that! But on the other hand we can't put up a notice to tell the audience where the scene is taking place, or change the set three or four times in each act.

**Leading Actor** That's what they used to do in the good old days.

**Producer** Yes, when the audience was about as bright as that little girl over there!

**Leading Actress** And it makes it easier to create an illusion.

**Father** (*leaping up*) An illusion? For pity's sake don't talk about illusions! Don't use that word, it's especially hurtful to us!

**Producer** (*astonished*) And why, for God's sake?

**Father** It's so hurtful, so cruel! You ought to have realised that!

**Producer** What else should we call it? That's what we do here – create an illusion for the audience . . .

**Leading Actor** With our performance . . .

**Producer** A perfect illusion of reality!

**Father** Yes, I know that, I understand. But on the other

hand, perhaps you don't understand as yet. I'm sorry! But you see, for you and for your actors what goes on here on the stage is, quite rightly, well, it's only a game.

**Leading Actress** (*interrupting indignantly*) A game! How dare you! We're not children! What happens here is serious!

**Father** I'm not saying that it isn't serious. And I mean, really, not just a game but an art, that tries, as you've just said, to create the perfect illusion of reality.

**Producer** That's right!

**Father** Now try to imagine that we, as you see us here, (*He indicates himself and the other* **Characters**.) that we have no other reality outside this illusion.

**Producer** (*astonished and looking at the* **Actors** *with the same sense of bewilderment as they feel themselves*) What the hell are you talking about now?

**Father** (*after a short pause as he looks at them, with a faint smile*) Isn't it obvious? What other reality is there for us? What for you is an illusion you create, for us is our only reality. (*Brief pause. He moves towards the* **Producer** *and goes on.*) But it's not only true for us, it's true for others as well, you know. Just think about it. (*He looks intently into the* **Producer***'s eyes.*) Do you really know who you are? (*He stands pointing at the* **Producer**.)

**Producer** (*a little disturbed but with a half-smile*) What? Who I am? I am me!

**Father** What if I told you that that wasn't true: what if I told you that you were me?

**Producer** I would tell you that you were mad!

*The* **Actors** *laugh.*

**Father** That's right, laugh! Because everything here is a game! (*To the* **Producer**.) And yet you object when I say that it is only for a game that the gentleman there (*Pointing* *to the* **Leading Actor**.) who is 'himself' has to be 'me', who, on the contrary, am 'myself'. You see, I've caught you in a trap.

*The* **Actors** *start to laugh.*

**Producer** Not again! We've heard all about this a little while ago.

**Father** No, no. I didn't really want to talk about this. I'd like you to forget about your game, (*Looking at the* **Leading Actress** *as if to anticipate what she will say.*) I'm sorry – your artistry! Your art! – that you usually pursue here with your actors; and I am going to ask you again in all seriousness, who are you?

**Producer** (*turning with a mixture of amazement and annoyance, to the* **Actors**) Of all the bloody nerve! A fellow who claims he is only a character comes and asks me who I am!

**Father** (*with dignity but without annoyance*) A character, my dear sir, can always ask a man who he is, because a character really has a life of his own, a life full of his own specific qualities, and because of these he is always 'someone'. While a man – I'm not speaking about you personally, of course, but man in general – well, he can be an absolute 'nobody'.

**Producer** All right, all right! Well, since you've asked me, I'm the Director, the Producer – I'm in charge! Do you understand?

**Father** (*half smiling, but gently and politely*) I'm only asking to try to find out if you really see yourself now in the same way that you saw yourself, for instance, once upon a time in the past, with all the illusions you had then, with everything inside and outside yourself as it seemed then – and not only seemed, but really was! Well then, look back on those illusions, those ideas that you don't have any more, on all those things that no longer seem the same to you. Don't you feel that not only this stage is falling away from under your feet but so is the earth itself, and that all these realities of today are going to seem tomorrow as if they had been an illusion?

**Producer** So? What does that prove?

**Father** Oh, nothing much. I only want to make you see that if we (*Pointing to himself and the other* **Characters**.) have no other reality outside our own illusion, perhaps you ought to distrust your own sense of reality: because whatever is a reality today, whatever you touch and believe in and that seems real for you today, is going to be – like the reality of yesterday – an illusion tomorrow.

**Producer** (*deciding to make fun of him*) Very good! So now you're saying that you as well as this play you're going to show me here, are more real than I am?

**Father** (*very seriously*) There's no doubt about that at all.

**Producer** Is that so?

**Father** I thought you'd realised that from the beginning.

**Producer** More real than I am?

**Father** If your reality can change between today and tomorrow –

**Producer** But everybody knows that it can change, don't they? It's always changing! Just like everybody else's!

**Father** (*crying out*) But ours doesn't change! Do you see? That's the difference! Ours doesn't change, it can't change, it can never be different, never, because it is already determined, like this, for ever, that's what's so terrible! We are an eternal reality. That should make you shudder to come near us.

**Producer** (*jumping up, suddenly struck by an idea, and standing directly in front of the* **Father**) Then I should like to know when anyone saw a character step out of his part and make a speech like you've done, proposing things, explaining things. Tell me when, will you? I've never seen it before.

**Father** You've never seen it because an author usually hides all the difficulties of creating. When the characters are alive, really alive and standing in front of their author, he has only to follow their words, the actions that they suggest to him: and he must want them to be what they want to be: and it's his bad luck if he doesn't do what they want! When a character is born he immediately assumes such an independence even of his own author that everyone can imagine him in scores of situations that his author hadn't even thought of putting him in, and he sometimes acquires a meaning that his author never dreamed of giving him.

**Producer** Of course I know all that.

**Father** Well, then. Why are you surprised by us? Imagine what a disaster it is for a character to be born in the imagination of an author who then refuses to give him life in a written script. Tell me if a character, left like this, suspended, created but without a final life, isn't right to do what we are doing now, here in front of you. We spent such a long time, such a very long time, believe me, urging our author, persuading him, first me, then her (*Pointing to the* **Stepdaughter**.), then this poor Mother . . .

**Stepdaughter** (*coming down the stage as if in a dream*) It's true, I would go, would go and tempt him, time after time, in his gloomy study just as it was growing dark, when he was sitting quietly in an armchair not even bothering to switch a light on but leaving the shadows to fill the room: the shadows were swarming with us, we had come to tempt him. (*As if she could see herself there in the study and is annoyed by the presence of the* **Actors**.) Go away will you! Leave us alone! Mother there, with that son of hers – me with the little girl – that poor little kid always on his own – and then me with him (*Pointing to the* **Father**.) and then at last, just me, on my own, all on my own, in the shadows. (*She turns quickly as if she wants to cling on to the vision she has of herself, in the shadows.*) Ah, what scenes, what scenes we suggested to him! What a life I could have had! I tempted him more than the others!

**Father** Oh yes, you did! And it was probably all your fault that he did nothing about it! You were so insistent, you made too many demands.

**Stepdaughter** But he wanted me to be like that! (*She comes closer to the* **Producer** *to speak to him in confidence.*) I think it's more likely that he felt discouraged about the theatre and even despised it because the public only wants to see . . .

**Producer** Let's get on, for God's sake, let's get on. Come to the point will you?

**Stepdaughter** I'm sorry, but if you ask me, we've got too much happening already, just with our entry into his house. (*Pointing to the* **Father**.) You said that we couldn't put up a notice or change the set every five minutes.

**Producer** Right! Of course we can't! We must combine things, group them together in one continuous flowing action: not the way you've been wanting, first of all seeing your little brother come home from school and wander about the house like a lost soul, hiding behind the doors and brooding on some plan or other that would – what did you say it would do?

**Stepdaughter** Wither him . . . shrivel him up completely.

**Producer** That's good! That's a good expression. And then you 'can see it there in his eyes, getting stronger all the time' – isn't that what you said?

**Stepdaughter** Yes, that's right. Look at him! (*Pointing to him as he stands next to his* **Mother**.)

**Producer** Yes, great! And then, at the same time, you want to show the little girl playing in the garden, all innocence. One in the house and the other in the garden – we can't do it, don't you see that?

**Stepdaughter** Yes, playing in the sun, so happy! It's the only pleasure I have left, her happiness, her delight in playing in the garden: away from the misery, the squalor of that sordid flat where all four of us slept and where she slept with me – with me! Just think of it! My vile, contaminated body close to hers, with her little arms wrapped tightly round my neck, so lovingly, so innocently. In the garden, whenever she saw me, she would run and take my hand. She never wanted to show me the big flowers, she would run about looking for the 'little weeny' ones, so that she could show them to me; she was so happy, so thrilled! (*As she says this, tortured by the memory, she breaks out into a long desperate cry, dropping her head on her arms that rest on a little table. Everybody is very affected by her. The* **Producer** *comes to her almost paternally and speaks to her in a soothing voice.*)

**Producer** We'll have the garden scene, we'll have it, don't worry: and you'll see, you'll be very pleased with what we do! We'll play all the scenes in the garden! (*He calls out to a* **Stage-hand** *by name.*) Hey . . . , let down a few bits of tree, will you? A couple of cypresses will do, in front of the fountain. (*Someone drops in the two cypresses and a* **Stage-hand** *secures them with a couple of braces and weights.*)

**Producer** (*to the* **Stepdaughter**) That'll do for now, won't it? It'll just give us an idea. (*Calling out to a* **Stage-hand** *by name again.*) Hey . . . , give me something for the sky will you?

**Stage-hand** What's that?

**Producer** Something for the sky! A small cloth to come in behind the fountain. (*A white cloth is dropped from the flies.*) Not white! I asked for a sky! Never mind: leave it! I'll do something with it. (*Calling out.*) Hey lights! Kill everything will you? Give me a bit of moonlight – the blues in the batten and a blue spot on the cloth . . . (*They do.*) That's it! That'll do! (*Now on the scene there is the light he asked for, a mysterious blue light that makes the* **Actors** *speak and move as if in the garden in the evening under a moon. To the* **Stepdaughter**.)

Look here now: the little boy can come out here in the garden and hide among the trees instead of hiding behind the doors in the house. But it's going to be difficult to find a little girl to play the scene with you where she shows you the flowers. (*Turning to the* **Little Boy**.) Come on, come on, son, come across here. Let's see what it'll look like. (*But the* **Boy** *doesn't move.*) Come on will you, come on. (*Then he pulls him forward and tries to make him hold his head up, but every time it falls down again on his chest.*) There's something very odd about this lad . . . What's wrong with him? My God, he'll have to say something some time! (*He comes over to him again, puts his hand on his shoulder and pushes him between the trees.*) Come a bit nearer: let's have a look. Can you hide a bit more? That's it. Now pop your head out and look round. (*He moves away to look at the effect and as the* **Boy** *does what he has been told to do, the* **Actors** *watch impressed and a little disturbed.*) Ahh, that's good, very good . . . (*He turns to the* **Stepdaughter**.) How about having the little girl, surprised to see him there, run across. Wouldn't that make him say something?

**Stepdaughter** (*getting up*) It's no use hoping he'll speak, not as long as that creature's there. (*Pointing to the* **Son**.) You'll have to get him out of the way first.

**Son** (*moving determinedly to one of the sets of steps leading off the stage*) With pleasure! I'll go now! Nothing will please me better!

**Producer** (*stopping him immediately*) Hey, no! Where are you going? Hang on!

*The* **Mother** *gets up, anxious at the idea that he is really going and instinctively raising her arms as if to hold him back, but without moving from where she is.*

**Son** (*at the footlights, to the* **Producer** *who is restraining him there*) There's no reason why I should be here! Let me go will you? Let me go!

**Producer** What do you mean there's no reason for you

to be here?

**Stepdaughter** (*calmly, ironically*) Don't bother to stop him. He won't go!

**Father** You have to play that terrible scene in the garden with your mother.

**Son** (*quickly, angry and determined*) I'm not going to play anything! I've said that all along! (*To the* **Producer**.) Let me go will you?

**Stepdaughter** (*crossing to the* **Producer**) It's all right. Let him go. (*She moves the* **Producer***'s hand from the* **Son**. *Then she turns to the* **Son** *and says.*) Well, go on then! Off you go!

*The* **Son** *stays near the steps but as if pulled by some strange force he is quite unable to go down them. Then to the astonishment and even the dismay of the* **Actors**, *he moves along the front of the stage towards the other set of steps down into the auditorium: but having got there, he again stays near and doesn't actually go down them. The* **Stepdaughter** *who has watched him scornfully but very intently, bursts into laughter.*

**Stepdaughter** He can't, you see? He can't! He's got to stay here! He must. He's chained to us for ever! No, I'm the one who goes, when what must happen does happen, and I run away, because I hate him, because I can't bear the sight of him any longer. Do you think it's possible for him to run away? He has to stay here with that wonderful father of his and his mother there. She doesn't think she has any other son but him. (*She turns to the* **Mother**.) Come on, come on, Mummy, come on! (*Turning back to the* **Producer** *to point her out to him.*) Look, she's going to try to stop him . . . (*To the* **Mother**, *half compelling her, as if by some magic power.*) Come on, come on. (*Then to the* **Producer** *again.*) Imagine how she must feel at showing her affection for him in front of your actors! But her longing to be near him is so strong that – look! She's going to go through that scene with him again! (*The* **Mother** *has now actually come close to the* **Son** *as the* **Stepdaughter** *says the last line: she* *gestures to show that she agrees to go on.*)

**Son** (*quickly*) But I'm not! I'm not! If I can't get away then I suppose I shall have to stay here; but I repeat that I will not have any part in it.

**Father** (*to the* **Producer**, *excitedly*) You must make him!

**Son** Nobody's going to make me do anything!

**Father** I'll make you!

**Stepdaughter** Wait! Just a minute! Before that, the little girl has to go to the fountain. (*She turns to take the* **Little Girl**, *drops on her knees in front of her and takes her face between her hands.*) My poor little darling, those beautiful eyes, they look so bewildered. You're wondering where you are, aren't you? Well, we're on a stage, my darling! What's a stage? Well, it's a place where you pretend to be serious. They put on plays here. And now we're going to put on a play. Seriously! Oh, yes! Even you . . . (*She hugs her tightly and rocks her gently for a moment.*) Oh, my little one, my little darling, what a terrible play it is for you! What horrible things have been planned for you! The garden, the fountain . . . Oh, yes, it's only a pretend fountain, that's right. That's part of the game, my pretty darling: everything is pretend here. Perhaps you'll like a pretend fountain better than a real one: you can play here then. But it's only a game for the others; not for you, I'm afraid, it's real for you, my darling, and your game is in a real fountain, a big beautiful green fountain with bamboos casting shadows, looking at your own reflection, with lots of baby ducks paddling about, shattering the reflections. You want to stroke one! (*With a scream that electrifies and terrifies everybody.*) No, Rosetta, no! Your mummy isn't watching you, she's over there with that selfish bastard! Oh, God, I feel as if all the devils in hell were tearing me apart inside . . . And you . . . (*Leaving the* **Little Girl** *and turning to the* **Little Boy** *in the usual way.*) What are you doing here, hanging about like a beggar? It'll be your fault too, if that little girl drowns; you're always like this, as if I wasn't paying the price for getting all of you into this house. (*Shaking his arm to make him take his hand out of his pocket.*) What have you got there? What are you hiding? Take it out, take your hand out! (*She drags his hand out of his pocket and to everyone's horror he is holding a revolver. She looks at him for a moment, almost with satisfaction, then she says, grimly.*) Where on earth did you get that? (*The* **Boy**, *looking frightened, with his eyes wide and empty, doesn't answer.*) You idiot, if I'd been you, instead of killing myself, I'd have killed one of those two: either or both, the father and the son. (*She pushes him towards the cypress trees where he then stands watching: then she takes the* **Little Girl** *and helps her to climb into the fountain, making her lie so that she is hidden; after that she kneels down and puts her head and arms on the rim of the fountain.*)

**Producer** That's good! It's good! (*Turning to the* **Stepdaughter**.) And at the same time . . .

**Son** (*scornfully*) What do you mean, at the same time? There was nothing at the same time! There wasn't any scene between her and me. (*Pointing to the* **Mother**.) She'll tell you the same thing herself, she'll tell you what happened.

*The* **Second Actress** *and the* **Juvenile Lead** *have left the group of* **Actors** *and have come to stand nearer the* **Mother** *and the* **Son** *as if to study them so as to play their parts.*

**Mother** Yes, it's true. I'd gone to his room . . .

**Son** Room, do you hear? Not the garden!

**Producer** It's not important! We've got to reorganise the events anyway. I've told you that already.

**Son** (*glaring at the* **Juvenile Lead** *and the* **Second Actress**) What do you want?

**Juvenile Lead** Nothing, I'm just watching.

**Son** (*turning to the* **Second Actress**) You as well! Getting ready to play her part are you? (*Pointing to the* **Mother**.)

**Producer** That's it. And I think you should be grateful –

they're paying you a lot of attention.

**Son** Oh, yes, thank you! But haven't you realised yet that you'll never be able to do this play? There's nothing of us inside you and you actors are only looking at us from the outside. Do you think we could go on living with a mirror held up in front of us that didn't only freeze our reflection for ever, but froze us in a reflection that laughed back at us with an expression that we didn't even recognise as our own?

**Father** That's right! That's right!

**Producer** (*to* **Juvenile Lead** *and* **Second Actress**) Okay. Go back to the others.

**Son** It's quite useless. I'm not prepared to do anything.

**Producer** Oh, shut up, will you, and let me listen to your mother. (*To the* **Mother**.) Well, you'd gone to his room, you said.

**Mother** Yes, to his room. I couldn't bear it any longer. I wanted to empty my heart to him, tell him about all the agony that was crushing me. But as soon as he saw me come in . . .

**Son** Nothing happened. I got away! I wasn't going to get involved. I never have been involved. Do you understand?

**Mother** It's true! That's right!

**Producer** But we must make up the scene between you, then. It's vital!

**Mother** I'm ready to do it! If only I had the chance to talk to him for a moment, to pour out all my troubles to him.

**Father** (*going to the* **Son** *and speaking violently*) You'll do it! For your Mother! For your Mother!

**Son** (*more than ever determined*) I'm doing nothing!

**Father** (*taking hold of his coat collar and shaking him*) For

God's sake, do as I tell you! Do as I tell you! Do you hear what she's saying? Haven't you any feelings for her?

**Son** (*taking hold of his* **Father**) No I haven't! I haven't! Let that be the end of it!

*There is a general uproar. The* **Mother** *frightened out of her wits, tries to get between them and separate them.*

**Mother** Please stop it! Please!

**Father** (*hanging on*) Do as I tell you! Do as I tell you!

**Son** (*wrestling with him and finally throwing him to the ground near the steps. Everyone is horrified*) What's come over you? Why are you so frantic? Do you want to parade our disgrace in front of everybody? Well, I'm having nothing to do with it! Nothing! And I'm doing what our author wanted as well – he never wanted to put us on the stage.

**Producer** Then why the hell did you come here?

**Son** (*pointing to the* **Father**) He wanted to, I didn't.

**Producer** But you're here now, aren't you?

**Son** He was the one who wanted to come and he dragged all of us here with him and agreed with you in there about what to put in the play: and that meant not only what had really happened, as if that wasn't bad enough, but what hadn't happened as well.

**Producer** All right, then, you tell me what happened. You tell me! Did you rush out of your room without saying anything?

**Son** (*after a moment's hesitation*) Without saying anything. I didn't want to make a scene.

**Producer** (*needling him*) What then? What did you do then?

**Son** (*he is now the centre of everyone's agonised attention and he crosses the stage*) Nothing . . . I went across the garden . . . (*He breaks off gloomy and absorbed.*)

**Producer** (*urging him to say more, impressed by his reluctance to speak*) Well? What then? You crossed the garden?

**Son** (*exasperated, putting his face into the crook of his arm*) Why do you want me to talk about it? It's horrible! (*The* **Mother** *is trembling with stifled sobs and looking towards the fountain.*)

**Producer** (*quietly, seeing where she is looking and turning to the* **Son** *with growing apprehension*) The little girl?

**Son** (*looking straight in front, out to the audience*) There, in the fountain . . .

**Father** (*on the floor still, pointing with pity at the* **Mother**) She was trailing after him!

**Producer** (*to the* **Son**, *anxiously*) What did you do then?

**Son** (*still looking out front and speaking slowly*) I dashed across. I was going to jump in and pull her out . . . But something else caught my eye: I saw something behind the tree that made my blood run cold: the little boy, he was standing there with a mad look in his eyes: he was standing looking into the fountain at his little sister, floating there, drowned.

*The* **Stepdaughter** *is still bent at the fountain hiding the* **Little Girl**, *and she sobs pathetically, her sobs sounding like an echo.*

*There is a pause.*

**Son** (*continuing*) I made a move towards him: but then . . .

*From behind the trees where the* **Little Boy** *is standing there is the sound of a shot.*

**Mother** (*with a terrible cry she runs along with the* **Son** *and all the* **Actors** *in the midst of a great general confusion*) My son! My son! (*And then from the confusion and crying her voice comes out.*) Help! Help me!

**Producer** (*amidst the shouting he tries to clear a space while the* **Little Boy** *is carried by his feet and shoulders behind the white skycloth.*) Is he wounded? Really wounded? (*Everybody except *the* **Producer** *and the* **Father** *who is still on the floor by the steps, has gone behind the skycloth and stays there talking anxiously. Then independently the* **Actors** *start to come back into view.*)

**Leading Actress** (*coming from the right, very upset*) He's dead! The poor boy! He's dead! What a terrible thing!

**Leading Actor** (*coming back from the left and smiling*) What do you mean, dead? It's all make-believe. It's a sham! He's not dead. Don't you believe it!

**Other Actors** (*from the right*) Make-believe? It's real! Real! He's dead!

**Other Actors** (*from the left*) No, he isn't. He's pretending! It's all make-believe.

**Father** (*running off and shouting at them as he goes*) What do you mean, make-believe? It's real! It's real, ladies and gentlemen! It's reality! (*And with desperation on his face he too goes behind the skycloth.*)

**Producer** (*not caring any more*) Make-believe?! Reality?! Oh, go to hell the lot of you! Lights! Lights! Lights!

*At once all the stage and auditorium is flooded with light. The* **Producer** *heaves a sigh of relief as if he has been relieved of a terrible weight and they all look at each other in distress and with uncertainty.*

**Producer** God! I've never known anything like this! And we've lost a whole day's work! (*He looks at the clock.*) Get off with you, all of you! We can't do anything now! It's too late to start a rehearsal. (*When the* **Actors** *have gone, he calls out.*) Hey, lights! Kill everything! (*As soon as he has said this, all the lights go out completely and leave him in the pitch dark.*) For God's sake!! You might have left the workers! I can't see where I'm going!

*Suddenly, behind the skycloth, as if because of a bad connection, a green light comes up to throw on the cloth a huge sharp shadow of the* **Characters**, *but without the* **Little Boy** *and the* **Little Girl**. *The* **Producer**, *seeing this, jumps off the stage, terrified. At the* *same time the flood of light on them is switched off and the stage is again bathed in the same blue light as before. Slowly the* **Son** *comes on from the right, followed by the* **Mother** *with her arms raised towards him. Then from the left, the* **Father** *enters.*

*They come together in the middle of the stage and stand there as if transfixed. Finally from the left the* **Stepdaughter** *comes on and moves towards the steps at the front: on the top step she pauses for a moment to look back at the other three and then bursts out in a raucous laugh, dashes down the steps and turns to look at the three figures still on the stage. Then she runs out of the auditorium and we can still hear her manic laughter out into the foyer and beyond.*

*After a pause the curtain falls slowly.*

# Notes

*page*

1 *Six Characters in Search of an Author*: the Italian carries the subtitle *commedia da fare*, which is often, but mistakenly, translated as 'comedy in the making'. *Commedia* means a play of any sort, while the sense of the other words is that the play is *to be made*, yet to be realised.

3 *the action of the play*: no indications of place or time are given. The action unfolds in anytown, anytime, outside history.

*Act One*

5 *the curtain is already up*: the theatre is in the state of disorder normal for a working session behind closed doors, not for a public performance. The sight of a stage with curtain up is common enough today, but was a shock for theatre-goers in the twenties and meant the shattering of the convention of the closed box with the 'fourth wall' which was required by traditional, nineteenth-century theatre. The fact of the unprepared stage changes the relationship between stage and stalls. The standard convention that the stage is a place where fictions unfold, where, for instance, people of modest background will pretend to be every inch a king, is jettisoned in favour of a theatre which is literally what it seems to be. The actual events take place on a stage, in real time.

*Prompter's box*: the prompter in the wings is still an accepted part of theatrical productions today, even if the task is now entrusted to an ASM (assistant stage manager), but he was an infinitely more conspicuous figure in Pirandello's day. Actors in Italy were not always required to learn their lines, but were permitted to repeat the words spoken aloud, in the hearing of the audience, by the prompter in the course of performance. This is the procedure which will be followed by the cast when they attempt to stage the characters' drama in Act Two. Pirandello was resolutely opposed to this practice, and insisted that his actors learn their lines so as to be independent of the prompter.

*'The Rules of the Game'*: the play in rehearsal, first performed in 1918, is by Pirandello himself. Often in English this has been replaced by *Hamlet*, presumably because Shakespeare's tragedy contains a play within a play, but Pirandello's choice was not arbitrary. A more literal translation of the play's Italian title would be *The Game of Parts*, or perhaps even *of Roles*, with the implication that men and women do not simply live their lives but play a part or act out a role. The play also focuses on the clash between seeming and reality, on the pain of the false 'mask' and even on the demands of society. Leone Gala, whose wife lives with another man, at her request passes an hour every day at her house so that the neighbours will have the impression that the proprieties of family life are still being respected. He is a subtle, detached, 'humorous', slightly cynical observer of life, who is aware of the grotesqueness of his situation and indeed of the 'mask' he is wearing. 'Yes I laugh sometimes as I watch myself in this self-imposed role,' he says. While experiencing little of the inner torment of the Father in *Six Characters in Search of an Author*, he is his precursor in his awareness of the dilemmas of imposed identity, or mask. The deep sense of the play is lost on the cast, who make jibes about the obscurity of Pirandello's writing, but the Producer, while joining in the laughter, is shrewd enough to unravel the sense of the work.

6 *'The Stage'*: a house magazine for actors and theatre professionals.

*The Producer*: the central figure in the production process, the one responsible for bringing the co-ordinating vision, more commonly nowadays called 'director'.

8 *Socrates*: the nickname given to Leone Gala's servant, Filippo. Gala has two main passions in life, cooking and philosophy, and Socrates is the uncomplaining audience for Gala's whimsical lectures.

*Guido Venanzi*: the lover of Silia, Gala's wife, and the man with whom she lives. The relations between the three men are relaxed, but after Silia is insulted by a group of louts, she pressurises her husband to challenge the ringleader to a duel to protect her honour. Leone issues the challenge, but insists that Venanzi is the real husband (the man who in fact wears the mask of husband), and must do the actual fighting. Venanzi is killed by his opponent.

*the directions as well?*: stage directions are not marginal in Pirandello, and the Producer, in insisting that the actors are made to grapple with the totality of the script, is ensuring that the author's wishes are respected. The prompter has a central role here.

*plays by Pirandello*: Pirandello was not a modest man, and had no hesitation in putting forward his own name, but ironically and playfully. He was conscious that the most common stricture on his plays was that they were unduly 'cerebral', and the Producer's interpretation of *The Rules of the Game*, for all its capricious humour, to some extent bears this out. The account of the symbolism of the yoke and white of an egg is not altogether fanciful.

9 *the Six Characters have come*: however they come on stage, this entrance marks the end of the first section of the play: the rehearsal will proceed no further. Pirandello attempted various styles of entrances. In the 1921 version of the play, the characters entered from backstage, that is, from the same place as the actors. Some critics suggested that this blurred the essential distinction between characters and actors. In the Paris

première in 1923, Georges Pitoëff had them descend on to the stage in an elevator. In Max Reinhardt's 1924 German production, the characters were on the stage from the beginning but hidden from view. It was only for the definitive 1925 version that Pirandello hit on the idea of having them enter down the aisles of the auditorium, escorted by the doorkeeper. This device guaranteed their separation from the actors on stage.

This means of making visible the distinction between characters and actors exercised Pirandello considerably, especially after reading criticism of the 1921 Italian production. Although he says that 'the most effective idea is to use masks', no director in recent times has adopted this technique. Nor did Pirandello himself when he directed the 1925 production with his own company. As a stage direction, the proposal to wear masks is a cogent metaphor for the fixed personality which a character, unlike a human being, possesses. Each character will be motivated by one 'fixed emotion', which Pirandello lists. He emphasises that the characters will be enveloped in an aura of mystery, but they must not appear as ghosts. They belong to a different level of being, but are not supernatural in the sense in which that word is normally used. They are imagined beings in a hierarchy in which 'beings' can be born as human, animal or even inanimate, and in which the human inventiveness can enlarge creation. (The characters are discussed individually in the section headed 'Characters and Characterisation'.)

11 *We're looking for an author*: the words are spoken without exaggeration or any attempt to create an artificial effect, but they express in a nutshell the substance of the characters' quest.

*We can be your new play*: the plural 'we' is significant. The conflicts between Father and Stepdaughter emerge later, but initially all six are united in a common quest.

*The Son stays sullenly behind*: even if the Father and Stepdaughter can find some unity, the Son remains detached and aloof, but this is an intrinsic part of his mask. His contempt is towards his family members and his resentment stems from being obliged willy-nilly to participate in their story.

12 *no need at all to pretend to be real because they are actually true*: the antithesis between being real and being true is one which engrossed Pirandello and which recurs frequently in his writing. The imaginative writer, or actor, has to strive to create an illusion of reality, or to coax the audience into a suspension of disbelief, but that illusion can only be brought about by a series of devices and tricks, whereas nature and life have no need of such efforts because they true in themselves. The Father's first assault on the Producer's reluctance to take an interest in him is through a discussion of theatre and of its paradoxes.

13 *thrust into life in many ways*: if life is a shapeless flux which is given manageable, comprehensible dimensions by having a form imposed on it, life can take many shapes at many levels – human, animal or even purely imaginative.

*a fantastic light*: the dialogue between Father and Producer can go only so far, but it has to be continually emphasised that the characters have their being in an unworldly sphere. They are not human beings.

*astonished and then indignant*: the Producer has to be won over gradually.

14 *Yes, that's right, we've been neglected . . .*: the Father is still the leading spokesperson for the six characters, and in this, the first of his philosophical monologues, he expatiates on the superiority of characters over human beings, since characters can never die.

*Sancho Panza . . . Prospero*: Sancho Panza is the companion of the wayward knight errant in Cervantes' novel, *Don Quixote*; Prospero is the deposed Duke of Milan and magician on the enchanted island in Shakespeare's *The Tempest*.

15 *It's in us, sir*: the characters are the play, and the play is the only life they can have, which explains their desperation to find an author to give them the prospect of living that life.

16 *Yes. It's worse . . . the traitor*: with this outburst, the Stepdaughter emerges in her own right as a rival to the Father for the attention of the Producer. Where he is ruggedly intellectual and deferential in his approach, she is all unrestrained passion and anger. At this point, the solidarity between the characters begins to disintegrate. They are united in their desire for life, but divided in the feelings they wish to express. The Stepdaughter offers the first, incomplete and tantalising, glimpses of the story which is in them. In all the discussion of ideas and passion, it is easy to overlook that Pirandello is a master theatrical craftsman in his manipulation of dramatic suspense.

17 *Is it real?*: even in minor points, like the Mother's fainting fit, the question of reality and illusion is present.

18 *She's not a woman, she's a mother*: this is neither a trivial distinction nor is it intended, in the Father's eyes, as a slur. The definition goes to the heart of this woman's being, and defines her mask and her drama. Hers is not intended as a torrid love story of a woman trapped in a loveless marriage and falling in doomed love with another man. Her drama concerns her relations with her children, and the failure of her son to return her affection for him.

*He made me go away with him!*: for the moment the Mother's story occupies centre stage. She portrays herself as passive, as obedient to her husband even when he is compelling her to fall short of her obligations as a wife and leave the home with another man. As a 'mother' she would not have contemplated such a thing.

19 *we're the audience*: there are always two audiences – the paying public and the actors on stage.

*the Daemon of Experiment*: the Son borrows terminology from the overblown speech of contemporary Decadent poets, notably Gabriele D'Annunzio (1863–1938). The Greek concept of *daimon* was an inner urge, a familiar spirit driving an exalted class of men to risk, adventure and heroism. This class of man could not be bound by convention or tradition. To the Son, this thought and expression of the Father's are no more than empty words.

*comfort in a word*: in a strange way, the Father is in agreement, but in his view words are indispensable for finding relief from unease of spirit. On this point, communication between the family is strained, as is all communication between human beings. As Pirandello had explained in his Preface, every human being uses words which refer to his own experience but these may not concur with the experience of others using identical terms.

*your sense of remorse*: the Stepdaughter's drive is to expose the Father's remorse as sham and to extract her own revenge for what he has done to her. The whole family turn on the Father, believing that his actions were determined by selfishness which he justifies to himself by bizarre, abstract reasoning not by genuine feeling.

*The money he was going to offer as payment*: the drama continues to emerge piecemeal, without context. The episode of the Stepdaughter's descent into prostitution horrifies the actors. The Stepdaughter's choice to blurt out these stray facts upsets the Son, who is never in agreement with his half-sister.

*Madame Pace*: the brothel-keeper who conceals her real activity by posing as a dressmaker is the only character in the play who is given a name. *Pace* is the Italian for peace; *Robes et Manteaux* dresses and coats in French.

20 *Why don't you put your foot down*: the Father treats the Producer with respect and concedes primacy in all matters theatrical to him.

22 *But I want to listen to this first*: in spite of his initial

scepticism and the continuing impatience of his actors, the Producer's interest is aroused. This change of attitude is a sign of the movement and change which occurs in the 'outer' play as well as in the drama of the Characters.

*Listen then*: the Father resumes his position as narrator. The story of the family is beginning to emerge in greater coherence, but is still being told in fits and starts.

23 *sound moral healthiness*: this belief is central to the Father's self-image and fundamental to his ongoing process of '*costruirsi*' (constructing himself – see p. xli). His narrative is an extended attempt at justifying and explaining himself, particularly as regards the one crucial, shaming encounter in Madame Pace's shop. The Stepdaughter's derisive laughter at this assertion is equally important to her assumed image.

25 *All this is off the point, you know*: the Italian original has more the sense that all that he has heard so far is, in the Producer's view, mere storytelling or narrative, and thus not theatre. This is confirmed by his next line when he voices his doubts over whether, even now that his curiosity is engaged, the story of the characters meets the requirements of the stage. In an article for the magazine *Marzocco* in 1899, Pirandello wrote: 'In our day, most dramatic works are essentially narrative, drawing their subject matter from novels or short stories. This can only be a mistake, principally because in general a narrative is not easily reducible to the proportions of the stage.' The Producer is perfectly Pirandellian in his reservations and he shows once again his own keen sense of the imperatives of stagecraft.

*The drama begins now*: all that has gone before is to be regarded as background material which had to be conveyed to the listeners to allow them to understand and appreciate the drama which is about to commence on stage. The story of the Father coercing the Mother to leave the family home, of the relationship between her and the secretary, of the birth of the other children is not the subject which the characters wish to dramatise. That concerns the encounter in Madame Pace's shop and its aftermath.

*As soon as my father died*: immediately the two main characters come to blows over the ownership of the story and the slant to be given to it. The Father does not allow her to complete the sentence.

26 *needs of my flesh*: the Father in his speeches on this subject, pleading for understanding and forgiveness, uses two levels of reasoning: (1) Pirandellian philosophy of the pain and injustice of an imposed mask – for him it is unfair that a lecherous mask has been imposed on account of one experience; (2) that he is a man and subject to the sexual urges of all males. This plea is cast in purely human terms, with no appeal to any sort of abstraction, Pirandellian or other.

27 *blushing shame of human bestiality*: this is a kind of speech far removed from any talk of 'daemons of experiment'. The Father does not glory in what he had done, or present his giving in to sexual appetite as proof of his superior status. Pirandello compared himself to D'Annunzio on this point, saying that while D'Annunzio 'is immoral in order to proclaim the glory of instinct, I present the individual case to add another proof of the tragedy of being human. D'Annunzio is exultant over evil: I grieve over it' (Vittorini, 1958, p. 261).

*crocodile tears!*: this is the most basic of all divides between the Father and the Stepdaughter. In her craving for revenge, she will leave him no vestige of dignity and regards as hypocritical his appeal to grand concepts.

29 *This is the real drama for me*: the drama for him is tied up with his enduring quest for forgiveness. On this occasion, his appeal is couched in philosophical (Pirandellian) terms. For him personality is not single but multiple, and he begs release from the tyranny and

injustice of having one aspect (mask) of his personality drown the more benevolent, humane aspects of his character. Being caught in one compromising situation on one occasion should not determine how he is viewed overall. That view, he says, is bad philosophy, because human beings are more complex.
*I don't come into it*: the clash between Son and Stepdaughter, rather than between Father and Stepdaughter, comes to the fore.

31 *not fully developed dramatically*: Pirandello writes in the Preface that the Son 'denies the drama which makes him a character', and 'lives solely as a "character in search of an author"' (p. 216). He strives to distance himself from the other members of his family.

33 *it might work*: the Producer has been won over by the arguments he has heard. It is he who will sketch out the order of scenes and see if the story can be realised theatrically.

34 *commedia dell'arte*: the theatrical tradition which held sway in Italy between, roughly, the mid-sixteenth and mid-eighteenth centuries. It was actor-, not writer-, centred and relied heavily on improvisation. The actors wore masks to denote the characters they were playing, which gave Pirandello the terminology of the 'mask and face'.

*Act Two*

35 *What do you mean, it doesn't matter?*: now that the issue of whether or not to produce the characters' drama has been settled, the question to be faced in this scene concerns theatre itself and the nature of theatrical illusion. Initially the Stepdaughter queries the accuracy of the setting in Madame Pace's back shop since for her these questions are central to her life, but the Producer brushes aside such quibbles as irrelevant.

38 *That woman is me?*: the Stepdaughter is voicing the same incredulity that the Father had just expressed with his line – 'what do you mean, a rehearsal?' Theatre and

life clash, but the Stepdaughter is also expressing doubts Pirandello had expressed in 1908 in his essay 'Illustrators, Actors and Translators'. 'No matter how much an actor tries to enter into the author's intentions, it will be hard for him to succeed in seeing as the author saw, in feeling as the author felt and in transferring on to a stage as the author would have wished' (Basnett and Lorch, p. 27). The Father and Stepdaughter are here in the place of the author, but the former is disconcerted to find that their life is about to be transferred into another medium by others, whatever their skills, and the latter simply baffled at the disparity between her and the actress who would play her. The point will be repeated by both as the actors start to perform. The actors are not inadequate as actors, but they are an intrusion to the main business of portraying an author's vision to his public.

42 *Madame Pace takes a few steps downstage*: with this entrance, all pretence at realism is shattered. Madame Pace makes an appearance because she is required for this scene. She is deliberately grotesque in costume, and is made comic in the original by the odd mixture of Spanish and Italian she adopts. She has no conception of being on stage and will speak quietly, and inaudibly for the audience, not in any 'stage whisper'.

44 *Here in the theatre you have to make yourself heard!*: the Producer makes a number of interventions on theatre conventions. The first, and obvious one, concerns the need to project the voice to an audience so they can hear the arrangements for what is about to occur between Stepdaughter and Father even if in reality they would not wish to be overheard.

46 *The Mother leaps up*: the scene, involving her daughter, jars with the Mother for whom this is life, not theatrical performance. Reality cannot be contained for her, nor her behaviour restrained.

47 *The Scene*: finally the characters impose their will, and the drama gets under way systematically. It is a lewd

tale of debauchery, involving male libertinism and female vulnerability. Many such tales involving prostitution had been written by realist writers.

49 *Don't put that last line down*: the Producer acts as censor. His awareness of contemporary conventions, which he does not challenge, means on this occasion that he will not permit any offence or risk alienating his respectable audiences. The style of delivery too will have to be transformed to make it acceptable, including making it 'a lot more light-hearted'. Anything too brutal, too shocking, too challenging is ruled out. Questions over what was acceptable in the name of realism were keenly debated at that time, and not only in Italy. G. B. Shaw with *Mrs Warren's Profession* and Ibsen with *Ghosts*, dealing with prostitution and venereal disease respectively, produced responses of splenetic outrage from those whose taste was offended by being told of such things. This call to order is also the moment when the characters again lose their hard-won autonomy and control. The Producer resumes the position of authority, moving the characters aside and re-introducing the actors on to the stage to redo theatrically what the characters had done spontaneously. This will lead to tensions between the two groups, with the Stepdaughter being especially scathing.

54 *Truth's all very well up to a point but . . .*: the conviction that there are limits to the truth that can be portrayed leads to the Stepdaughter's fear that her drama will be reduced to 'a sugary little sentimental romance'. At this point, the confrontation is not between art and life but between concepts of theatre. The Producer will impose his authority since for all his sympathy for the Stepdaughter, he believes that he 'can't really put a scene like that on the stage'.

55 *Now we're getting to the real truth*: as well as acting as moral censor, the Producer has to arbitrate between the two characters who each want to use the stage to portray only their individual point of view, while he

wants to portray the clash by balancing the demands of each. His knowledge of the workings of drama cannot be faulted.

58 *Scream, Mummy, scream*: the scream is the interface between reality and the theatre, but in the drama the timely arrival of the Mother fends off the unthinkable horror of near-incest, which might have been indeed too much even for realist theatre.

*Act Three*

60 *When the curtain goes up*: it had been lowered by mistake, giving a plausible closure to the previous act, but the stage now reveals that the characters' drama is still commanding the attention of the theatre professionals. The setting is being prepared for a scene in the garden of the Father's house, in which the 'two' families are now unhappily cohabiting. The Stepdaughter now has the upper hand over the Father, and the Son is distant and resentful, to the pained regret of the Mother. The Father takes refuge in words and abstractions.

63 *so is the earth itself*: no truth, no belief can be held as certain and beyond doubt. Pirandello was one of an iconoclastic generation who pulled down the pillars which had held erect a whole system of previously unquestioned values and convictions. The human being is left alone, uncertain and fearful in a world he had once commanded. His certainties and beliefs, once corroborated by religion, are shown to be phoney swindles. Not even his sense of the reality of himself and his surrounding universe can be trusted any more. As the Father tells the Producer, the earth is crumbling beneath his feet.

65 *You've never seen it because an author . . .*: the moments of reflection and the spurts of action are cleverly timed in this final act. The last encounter between the three main protagonists centres on a meditation on theatre, allowing them to ruminate on the nature of creativity,

the autonomy of the character from the author who creates him and the reasons why 'their' author should have refused them life.

66 *Yes, playing in the sun, so happy!*: switch of attention back to the drama of the characters. The Little Girl is near the pool in a representation of the garden in the Father's house. The characters unobtrusively take over to act out their final scene.

67 *batten*: wooden bar.

72 *living with a mirror*: Pirandello's theatre was often tagged 'theatre of the mirror'. The reflection of the image, or double image of being and seeming, was intolerable for those who preferred simply to live without having to examine their life.

73 *to parade our disgrace*: the Son is compelled, against his wishes, to play his part, but the Italian has him complaining that the Father has no compunction over displaying 'his and our' shame. The Son's refusal is two-sided, both at being involved in theatre at all and at being humiliated by his family.

75 *Make-believe? It's real!*: the dilemma raised by the characters' appearance is still unresolved.
*workers*: lights which remain on when the theatre is dark.
*Suddenly, behind a skycloth*: the six characters do not exit together as they had entered. The Boy and Girl are absent, and the Stepdaughter runs off on her own, meaning that the original 'legitimate' family has been reconstructed. The father of the other three children is dead, and the three children of that union are separated from the original nucleus, which resumes its own life. The cycle of the family drama is complete.

# Questions for Further Study

1 Discuss the different conflicts which form the structure of *Six Characters in Search of an Author.*
2 How do the Producer's views of the six characters and their untold story develop?
3 Why does Pirandello write in his introduction that to express the deep sense of the play the six characters ought to wear masks? What are the implications of this advice for a director?
4 What does Pirandello mean when he has the Father say of the Mother 'She is not a woman, she's a mother'?
5 Do you view the Producer as a man whose limited imagination and conventional views make him hostile to innovation in drama, or as a theatre-maker with a keen awareness of audience expectations and of the nature of his craft?
6 Are the Father and the Stepdaughter always in opposition to each other?
7 What makes the Father, a character, feel entitled to ask the Producer, a human being, who he is?
8 What is the basis of the Father's resentment of the Stepdaughter's contemptuous opinion of him?
9 How clear does the 'play within the play', that is, the inner drama of the six characters, become?
10 Do any of the characters or people in *Six Characters in Search of an Author* engage the audience's sympathy in the way that would normally occur in theatre?
11 How important is the Mother in the unravelling of the total action of *Six Characters in Search of an Author*?
12 To what extent does *Six Characters in Search of an Author* display Pirandello's views on the clash, mentioned in his introduction, between 'the face and the mask'?
13 In his introduction, Pirandello spoke of the problems of

communication based as it is on the 'empty abstraction of words'. Is this problem apparent throughout the unfolding drama?

14 What makes it difficult for the Father and the Stepdaughter to accept the performances of the actors chosen to depict them?

15 Are the actors merely bystanders to the main action of the play?

16 Is the sudden, semi-magical appearance of Madame Pace merely a striking stage effect?

17 What makes the non-speaking parts of the children vital to the overall work?

18 Discuss why, in your view, it is only the *original* family, without the offspring of the relationship between the Mother and the secretary, who appear together at the conclusion of the play.

19 Do you accept the frequently voiced criticism that *Six Characters in Search of an Author* is an unduly cerebral or over-intellectualised piece of theatre writing?

20 'The quest for the reasons why Pirandello denied life to his six characters is simultaneously intriguing, futile and intellectually risky' (Samuel Thomson). Do you agree with this judgement?

## Methuen Drama Student Editions

Jean Anouilh *Antigone* • John Arden *Serjeant Musgrave's Dance* Alan Ayckbourn *Confusions* • Aphra Behn *The Rover* • Edward Bond *Lear* • *Saved* • Bertolt Brecht *The Caucasian Chalk Circle* • *Fear and Misery in the Third Reich* • *The Good Person of Szechwan* • *Life of Galileo* • *Mother Courage and her Children* • *The Resistible Rise of Arturo Ui* • *The Threepenny Opera* • Anton Chekhov *The Cherry Orchard* • *The Seagull* • *Three Sisters* • *Uncle Vanya* • Caryl Churchill *Serious Money* • *Top Girls* • Shelagh Delaney *A Taste of Honey* • Euripides *Elektra* • *Medea* • Dario Fo *Accidental Death of an Anarchist* • Michael Frayn *Copenhagen* • John Galsworthy *Strife* • Nikolai Gogol *The Government Inspector* • Robert Holman *Across Oka* • Henrik Ibsen *A Doll's House* • *Ghosts* • *Hedda Gabler* • Charlotte Keatley *My Mother Said I Never Should* • Bernard Kops *Dreams of Anne Frank* • Federico García Lorca *Blood Wedding* • *Doña Rosita the Spinster* (bilingual edition) • *The House of Bernarda Alba* • (bilingual edition) • *Yerma* (bilingual edition) • David Mamet *Glengarry Glen Ross* • *Oleanna* • Patrick Marber *Closer* • John Marston *Malcontent* • Martin McDonagh *The Lieutenant of Inishmore* • Joe Orton *Loot* • Luigi Pirandello *Six Characters in Search of an Author* • Mark Ravenhill *Shopping and F***ing* • Willy Russell *Blood Brothers* • *Educating Rita* • Sophocles *Antigone* • *Oedipus the King* • Wole Soyinka *Death and the King's Horseman* • Shelagh Stephenson *The Memory of Water* • August Strindberg *Miss Julie* • J. M. Synge *The Playboy of the Western World* • Theatre Workshop *Oh What a Lovely War* Timberlake Wertenbaker *Our Country's Good* • Arnold Wesker *The Merchant* • Oscar Wilde *The Importance of Being Earnest* • Tennessee Williams *A Streetcar Named Desire* • *The Glass Menagerie*

## Methuen Drama Modern Plays

*include work by*

Edward Albee
Jean Anouilh
John Arden
Margaretta D'Arcy
Peter Barnes
Sebastian Barry
Brendan Behan
Dermot Bolger
Edward Bond
Bertolt Brecht
Howard Brenton
Anthony Burgess
Simon Burke
Jim Cartwright
Caryl Churchill
Complicite
Noël Coward
Lucinda Coxon
Sarah Daniels
Nick Darke
Nick Dear
Shelagh Delaney
David Edgar
David Eldridge
Dario Fo
Michael Frayn
John Godber
Paul Godfrey
David Greig
John Guare
Peter Handke
David Harrower
Jonathan Harvey
Iain Heggie
Declan Hughes
Terry Johnson
Sarah Kane
Charlotte Keatley
Barrie Keeffe
Howard Korder
Robert Lepage
Doug Lucie
Martin McDonagh
John McGrath
Terrence McNally
David Mamet
Patrick Marber
Arthur Miller
Mtwa, Ngema & Simon
Tom Murphy
Phyllis Nagy
Peter Nichols
Sean O'Brien
Joseph O'Connor
Joe Orton
Louise Page
Joe Penhall
Luigi Pirandello
Stephen Poliakoff
Franca Rame
Mark Ravenhill
Philip Ridley
Reginald Rose
Willy Russell
Jean-Paul Sartre
Sam Shepard
Wole Soyinka
Simon Stephens
Shelagh Stephenson
Peter Straughan
C. P. Taylor
Theatre Workshop
Sue Townsend
Judy Upton
Timberlake Wertenbaker
Roy Williams
Snoo Wilson
Victoria Wood

**Methuen Drama Contemporary Dramatists**
*include*

John Arden (two volumes)
Arden & D'Arcy
Peter Barnes (three volumes)
Sebastian Barry
Dermot Bolger
Edward Bond (eight volumes)
Howard Brenton (two volumes)
Richard Cameron
Jim Cartwright
Caryl Churchill (two volumes)
Sarah Daniels (two volumes)
Nick Darke
David Edgar (three volumes)
David Eldridge
Ben Elton
Dario Fo (two volumes)
Michael Frayn (three volumes)
David Greig
John Godber (four volumes)
Paul Godfrey
John Guare
Lee Hall (two volumes)
Peter Handke
Jonathan Harvey (two volumes)
Declan Hughes
Terry Johnson (three volumes)
Sarah Kane
Barrie Keeffe
Bernard-Marie Koltès (two volumes)
Franz Xaver Kroetz
David Lan
Bryony Lavery
Deborah Levy
Doug Lucie
David Mamet (four volumes)
Martin McDonagh
Duncan McLean
Anthony Minghella (two volumes)
Tom Murphy (six volumes)
Phyllis Nagy
Anthony Neilsen (two volumes)
Philip Osment
Gary Owen
Louise Page
Stewart Parker (two volumes)
Joe Penhall (two volumes)
Stephen Poliakoff (three volumes)
David Rabe (two volumes)
Mark Ravenhill (two volumes)
Christina Reid
Philip Ridley
Willy Russell
Eric-Emmanuel Schmitt
Ntozake Shange
Sam Shepard (two volumes)
Wole Soyinka (two volumes)
Simon Stephens (two volumes)
Shelagh Stephenson
David Storey (three volumes)
Sue Townsend
Judy Upton
Michel Vinaver (two volumes)
Arnold Wesker (two volumes)
Michael Wilcox
Roy Williams (three volumes)
Snoo Wilson (two volumes)
David Wood (two volumes)
Victoria Wood

**Methuen Drama World Classics**
*include*

Jean Anouilh (two volumes)
Brendan Behan
Aphra Behn
Bertolt Brecht (eight volumes)
Büchner
Bulgakov
Calderón
Čapek
Anton Chekhov
Noël Coward (eight volumes)
Feydeau (two volumes)
Eduardo De Filippo
Max Frisch
John Galsworthy
Gogol
Gorky (two volumes)
Harley Granville Barker (two volumes)
Victor Hugo
Henrik Ibsen (six volumes)
Jarry
Lorca (three volumes)
Marivaux
Mustapha Matura
David Mercer (two volumes)
Arthur Miller (six volumes)
Molière
Musset
Peter Nichols (two volumes)
Joe Orton
A. W. Pinero
Luigi Pirandello
Terence Rattigan (two volumes)
W. Somerset Maugham (two volumes)
August Strindberg (three volumes)
J. M. Synge
Ramón del Valle-Inclán
Frank Wedekind
Oscar Wilde

## Methuen Drama Classical Greek Dramatists

*Aeschylus Plays: One*
(Persians, Seven Against Thebes, Suppliants, Prometheus Bound)

*Aeschylus Plays: Two*
(Oresteia: Agamemnon, Libation-Bearers, Eumenides)

*Aristophanes Plays: One*
(Acharnians, Knights, Peace, Lysistrata)

*Aristophanes Plays: Two*
(Wasps, Clouds, Birds, Festival Time, Frogs)

*Aristophanes & Menander: New Comedy*
(Women in Power, Wealth, The Malcontent, The Woman from Samos)

*Euripides Plays: One*
(Medea, The Phoenician Women, Bacchae)

*Euripides Plays: Two*
(Hecuba, The Women of Troy, Iphigeneia at Aulis, Cyclops)

*Euripides Plays: Three*
(Alkestis, Helen, Ion)

*Euripides Plays: Four*
(Elektra, Orestes, Iphigeneia in Tauris)

*Euripides Plays: Five*
(Andromache, Herakles' Children, Herakles)

*Euripides Plays: Six*
(Hippolytos, Suppliants, Rhesos)

*Sophocles Plays: One*
(Oedipus the King, Oedipus at Colonus, Antigone)

*Sophocles Plays: Two*
(Ajax, Women of Trachis, Electra, Philoctetes)

